THE LAKE OF TWO RIVERS

DEC/2013

LLOYD & CAROL

I HOPE YOU ENJOY
THE STORIES!

Rolf Eliason

rolf-eliason@rogers.com

THE LAKE OF TWO RIVERS

ROLF ELIASON

COPYRIGHT © 2013 BY ROLF ELIASON.

LIBRARY OF CONGRESS CONTROL NUMBER:		2013915069
ISBN:	HARDCOVER	978-1-4836-8783-4
	SOFTCOVER	978-1-4836-8782-7
	EBOOK	978-1-4836-8784-1

All rights reserved. No part of this book may be reproduced or transmitted in any form or by any means, electronic or mechanical, including photocopying, recording, or by any information storage and retrieval system, without permission in writing from the copyright owner.

This book was printed in the United States of America.

Rev. date: 08/27/2013

To order additional copies of this book, contact:
Xlibris LLC
1-888-795-4274
www.Xlibris.com
Orders@Xlibris.com

CONTENTS

Preface 7
Acknowledgments 9

Chapter One: Keep It Simple 11
Chapter Two: The Wizard of Cause 27
Chapter Three: What Are You Doing with Your Life? 35
Chapter Four: The Lake of Two Rivers 47
Chapter Five: The Plain, Simple Truth 56
Chapter Six: Financial Enemies 66
Chapter Seven: Slay the Dragon 77
Chapter Eight: +PIT, −FIT 89
Chapter Nine: Anything Can Happen Anytime 98
Chapter Ten: What Really Counts? 108
Chapter Eleven: Out of the Fry Pan 119
Chapter Twelve: Up the Chimney 131

People, Books, and Companies Index 141
Topic Index 143

Preface

Have you ever considered the value of mentorship? Most people can think of one or more persons in their life that have made a significant contribution to their personal development. I am no different. However, having been raised in a small rural town in Western Canada, some might wish to call me a "Red Neck".

I would rather put a positive spin on it and say that I have strong opinions. You will certainly find in this book I love to tell stories. Why the Viking hat? You will understand later in the book.

Through mentorship and observing life stories, I realize personal finance is not as complicated as some make it out to be. This book encapsulates that mentorship I have experienced. These stories are noted in the form of plain, simple truth.

I encourage you to pass that same kind of mentorship on to people you love. It will have a positive, certain effect on their financial destination. With this, I hope to awaken your curiosity.

I also hope you enjoy the stories.

Acknowledgments

Many authors are quick to first acknowledge their significant other. I am no different, and this isn't just protocol. Joan, our life together has transformed me into the financial advisor and man that I am. Thank you.

Through our love, we produced two boys that have grown into young men any parent would be proud of. It was only a few memorable exchanges between father and son that spawned the writing of this book.

The mentorship of my late father-in-law, William Hopkins, to me has been priceless and must be mentioned. The effect that man had upon my development will become evident as you continue to read *The Lake of Two Rivers*. His balance between work and play to me was a definite inspiration.

I also would like to thank my sister, Sharon Miller, for assisting with primary editing. She was quick to point out what a past participle and prepositional phrase is. I had long forgotten.

Thank you to my clients for sharing their hopes, dreams, and experiences. I highly value these types of dialogue. Together, through dialogue we grow.

Finally, I would like to thank Xlibris publishers for the independence they have given me and the support to make the process of bringing my work to print a comfortable, professional, and enjoyable experience.

Chapter One

Keep It Simple

Not another book on personal finance!

This is a book on sizzle, not on steak. It is not just another book on personal finance but a collection of plain, simple truths, anecdotes and stories collected over a lifetime. I believe these stories and simple truths will have a strong positive effect on your financial direction if habits needing attention are addressed. If you are looking for guidance on complicated investment schemes, please look elsewhere. You will not find any here. This is a book focused on benefits. Yours!

The title of this chapter was chosen from a principle taught to me in a sales course taken many years ago. It is called the KISS principle. Keep it simple and supported. Not only do I wish to focus on benefits (they will be referred to as sizzle), I also wish to arouse your curiosity. Just as the map you refer to on a journey will have a significant bearing on your destination, I believe this collection of anecdotes and stories will inspire you to take appropriate action that will positively affect your financial direction and future.

Having an appropriate plan is not enough. You may already have wonderful plans, but you may not be reaching your expectations. That is, if you have a plan. However, without appropriate action nothing will happen. You may actually have to do something, such as alter your financial habits. That plan must be applied to your life with zeal and determination.

Time is precious to everyone, and it is my best guess you are wondering in the back of your mind if spending the time reading this book will be worth the effort. Will I learn anything of value? Just look around the business section of the bookstore, and you will find dozens of books on personal finance. What makes this one special?

As a former industrial sales representative, I would bet you are not so much interested in features or advantages of a particular investment strategy. I would bet strongly what is actually in the back of your mind is benefit: *What is reading this material going to do for me? Do I really foresee any change in my finances after reading this?*

I have spent several years in postsecondary education and almost twenty years in various technical sales capacities within the province of Ontario. I am now entering my fifteenth year in personal finance as an advisor and have been managing my own household portfolio of capital for about twice that length of time.

However, what I believe to be of significance is having listened to the life stories of many people, including their hopes, fears, aspirations, and life situations. This has given me inspiration in a direct way. This is what I believe truly matters: *providing plain, simple truth extracted from actual life experience.* It has been through lessons learned through heroes of mine that I feel compelled to give back.

Rocket science it is not

Let me provide clarity here. There is no magic. This is not a get-rich-quick scheme. The world is full of hucksters and Ponzi schemes. Many of these purveyors of financial advice, while self-serving, have been crucified in the media and are now in jail. *Ponzi scheme* has become a common household phrase. We understand the phrase "Bernie that *made off* with the loot!" Thank goodness he got jail time, and rightly so! The relationship between an investor and a financial advisor is a fiduciary relationship, which means the advisor must place the investor's interest ahead of himself or herself. Period! To treat another person the same way you would have that person treat you, as the golden rule states.

A wallet versus a badge

My wife and I have two sons of whom we are very proud. At the time of writing, Carl, the older of the two, is a commercial pilot in Northern Ontario, and Evan, the younger of the two, is entering third-year law. I approached Evan one day and asked him a loaded question: "Which would you rather have, a big badge or a big wallet?" I was proud of his choice—the wallet, of course. The point that I bring to bear is there are many cowboys out there with a big hat but no cattle. They seem to have lots of ideas but nothing to show for it. All bark, with no bite. Another familiar saying goes "Money talks!" But isn't it better to have both the hat *and* the cattle? You tell me!

A collection of thoughts thirty-three years in the making

Let's talk turkey. In no way am I downplaying the value of education, but I have seen many highly educated people with plenty of ideas but not having two nickels to rub together. How can this be? My father was often noted to break silence in a business meeting with a raised hand, rubbing his thumb and index finger together in the air while saying quietly, "Show me the money!" The fact is that sooner or later, ideas need funding. Expenses must be paid. Programs require capital. Life is expensive.

One day you may choose not to work. If that decision is postponed, the time will eventually come when you will no longer have capacity to perform tasks required in your work. This may be for whatever reason, be it sickness, health, or family. For some, this change is realized sooner than for others. The real question is, from where will payments for continuing expenses come? Would the payments come from your line of credit? Are you kidding? It seems to me our banks in the last ten years have been very adept at selling home equity lines of credit, complete with a Robin Hood Flour type of application: *general purpose*.

What? You didn't get to your Caribbean holiday? Why not just put it on the line of credit? While signing you up for the line of credit, advocates for these lines of credit don't seem to focus on the fact that they have a vested interest in signing you up. They may not specifically tell you to use the home equity line of credit for use on personal-use property, trips, or other financial sinkholes, but there is a definite implication of easy money. Come on, get real! Business continues only where profit is made.

Fortunately, at the relatively young age of twenty-five I had wonderful financial counsel. Even though I may not have been a rocket scientist, I was smart enough to listen to someone smarter than I. At the time of writing, this would make over thirty years of investing and collection of thoughts. These thoughts have felt like a pressure pot of ideas just waiting to explode. So here we go . . .

Let's just call it investing 101

There are many successful investors out there. The one most likely to come to mind is Warren Buffett. Undoubtedly he is by far the most famous investor today, and we are fortunate to live concurrently with the man to observe his habits. He is one to be emulated—financially, of course. He is a value investor. He looks for stocks on sale at a low price. After purchasing at a very low price, and as an owner, he then waits very patiently. His homework was done long before the purchase.

Wayne Gretzky is undoubtedly the Great One of Hockey, and more will be said of him later. Wayne truly has the game of hockey figured out. Likewise, Warren Buffett is also the Great One—but in the game of *investment*. Many people are fans of his style of investing. You only have to attend one of the Berkshire Hathaway meetings in Omaha, Nebraska, to observe several thousand enthusiastic investors living off every word the man speaks to understand his popularity. When speaking with clients, I often use a few of his quick quotes. I encourage you to Google them. His quips are awesome! For example, his number 1 rule is not to lose money. Rule number 2 is not to forget rule number 1. To say the least, Mr. Buffett knows well the value of downside protection.

I often ask, "If your portfolio goes down 25 percent in one year, how much do you have to make to get back to your starting point?" The answer is not 25 percent. The answer is 33⅓ percent. How can that be? When you drop 25 percent, you now have 75 percent of your holdings to work on. To get back the 25 percent lost, you must make one-third of the 75 percent you are now at to make it back to 100 percent. This equals 33⅓ percent of where you now are.

I believe this to be the very reason Mr. Buffett chose this rule. Why? *It is more difficult to make money on lost money than on a previously larger base.* And this truth works in an exponential fashion. If you lose 50 percent of your money, you would have to make 100 percent return to get back to where you started. If you lose 10 percent, you have only to make 11 percent to return to square one. Downside protection is more important than you may realize.

Two components of investing: risk and return

Most investors are eager to track the return on their investments but have little or no idea of the risk they are taking to achieve that return. Many investors understand the idea of rolling the dice and the randomness in the result of rolling die, but give little thought to how risky or safe their particular investment is or what particular risk or risks they are actually facing. Some investments, in their minds, are deemed safe when there is no understanding of the risk that investment is exposed to.

Let's explore an example: guaranteed investment certificates. They are guaranteed by the Canadian Deposit Insurance Company to pay back principal and interest posted to a maximum of $100,000 per company, even if the supplier goes bankrupt. This is better than cash on yield, but they are somewhat illiquid. There is a locked-in period. So is there any risk at all? Not in their mind. One could argue opportunity cost—what one might have received if invested elsewhere—but what risk is specific to the certificates that one might not be accounting for? First of all, a real rate of return is adjusted for both taxation and inflation. It is not the numbers in the bank that count. It is what those numbers will buy that truly matters.

I am old enough to remember buying a deluxe hamburger back in my little hometown in Wetaskiwin, Alberta, at Hannigan's for thirty-five cents as a young teenager. That's right, thirty-five cents! This was a pile of cash for a teenager back then. 'Twas the best burger in the West! Mmmm, I love fried onions! Thank you, Mr. Hannigan! Better yet, it was Alberta beef smothered with all the trimmings. You wouldn't be able to buy the same type of burger for ten times that price today. And that is the silent killer of making money. The culprit is not the burger. It is losing your hard-earned money to purchasing power, courtesy of inflation.

In the case of GICs, these certificates in a nonregistered account are also subject to taxation each year. The break-even point, or point at which you start to make an increase on purchasing power, is expressed in this mathematical equation:

> The yearly inflation (or percentage change in the year to year rate of consumer price index) divided by (one minus your marginal tax rate).

Your marginal tax rate is the percentage of the next dollar that you earn that goes to Revenue Canada in taxation. This means that if you had a presumed inflation rate of 2 percent and a marginal tax rate of 35 percent, the break-even point at which you would start making any kind of real tax-adjusted rate of return is expressed mathematically as $2 / (1 - 0.35) = 3.08\%$.

What kind of GIC is paying 3.08 percent today? True, it would bode well in the event of a market crash, but you may be making even less than you realize after taxes and inflation are taken into account. It is very important to look at *all risks you are exposed to*, not just the ones talked about. These are risks that may not be discussed by the person at the desk where they are sold.

Taxation and inflation

Now please don't get me wrong. If the market is going to hell in a handbasket, my opinion is, in the event of a market crash, cash would then be a great place to park your holdings until after the fall. The problem is that no one can predict if and when the fall occurs. Locking your money into a period of time within a GIC will yield marginally higher for the inconvenience of the locked-in term you face. However, it is my argument that *neither of these instruments take care of the risk of taxation and inflation you are subject to.* Between stocks, bonds, and cash, cash—when faced with a market crash—is like grabbing onto the bush on the side of the river instead of going over the falls! Would I have liked to be in cash when the credit crisis of 2008 hit?

Here's a place money is made

Before answering this question, I digress just a little bit. Let me remind you of the time when our beloved banks actually believed the bond rating services. It was before summertime, 2008. I'm going to let you in on a little secret: *banks make money, and plenty of it.* One of the ways they make money is by bundling up debt and reselling it to other financial institutions in the form of commercial paper at a higher interest rate than the underlying debt instruments.

They're rubbing their hands together

"Shouldn't we buy some commercial paper? Let's buy hundreds of millions of dollars of it. Are we ever going to make money! There is hardly any risk involved, and boy, the yield will make us look like heroes! Better yet, it has been rated double A+ by the bond rating services. These bond rating guys really are the professionals!" As an aside, one of the five major Canadian banks had a pile of the mortgage-backed securities at one point but got out before D-day. Was that luck, or was that foresight? I can't answer that. The other four were up to their necks in commercial paper ownership when the unexpected crunch came.

ROLF ELIASON

Bankers at lunch

Meanwhile, back in New York City at lunch, a bond rater says to a commercial banker after two martinis each, "Maybe we were off just a little on the commercial paper risk. Instead of double A, we have now revised it to double B-minus. Just a little bitty adjustment."

Two more martinis each later, the banker says to another banker present, "I'm not buying this bundled-up mortgage debt any longer. It's too risky! What if interest rates go up and we have a bunch of liar loans? Something smells toxic to me. Besides, I'm not so sure Fannie Mae or Freddie Mac necessarily got the truth from the truck driver on his actual level of income. *Maybe he should have bought a little smaller house.* Even though Fannie and Freddie earned their commission from selling those mortgages, I'm not buying any more of it. I smell bundled-up mortgage defaults coming down the road, driven by liar loans!"

The other banker says, "Well, if you're not buying it, then neither am I!" Almost instantly, the banks have no liquidity. No more loans, period! That would be a message from the really big guys high up in the banks. The banks, like Mr. Buffett, do not like to lose money either.

Keep them happy

There is a saying "In the economy, if the banks ain't happy, ain't nobody happy!" That might spell economic chaos, and some big politicians might even lose their jobs! I think we all remember President Obama quickly getting out the big checkbook. Seven hundred thousand times a million dollars equals *$700 billion the check was written for.*

Seven hundred what?

Most people can't even imagine a million dollars, let alone a billion. Well, for starters, let's count to one thousand, and every number you count is a million dollars. Then, do what you just did seven hundred times! This is almost beyond belief. It is even more difficult to understand what went on when you break it down. At the same time, the US National Debt was around $13 *trillion*. That would be thirteen thousand times a billion dollars. Now at the time of writing, it is just below $17 trillion. We will touch more on that later.

It was September 2008. All the while, the toxic assets purchased by the banks had to, in some way or another, be written off. "Hmmm, this is not going to be good for the shareholders to view. Wait a minute! That check written by Obama was from the account of the average taxpayer. That gets us off the hook!" It reminds me of my cartoon hero, Old Quick Draw McGraw: "Yippee-i-oh-kayee, gallopin' all the way . . ." Sickening, isn't it?

What about ties?

Now, I ask you the question, were enough strings attached to the gift to the banks by the president? Was the president emulating my cartoon hero, Old Quick Draw? You decide! I mention your need to focus on the lucrative subsequent retirement packages for senior bankers that quickly followed. I can't believe heads have yet to roll at the bond rating services.

Wasn't it John the Baptist that ended up with his head on a platter? And he didn't even lose anyone's money! Is there some kind of connection between the banks and the bond rating services? Perhaps there are a lot of relatives between each shop? I just can't decide on that one. The rest of the picture to me seems clear.

Let's go back to GICs. Would I have liked to have been in cash or GICs when the 2008 crisis hit? Absolutely! But was I personally there? No, I wasn't. I, like most investors, took a beating over the falls. But this brings me to my next point. No one has a crystal ball. It is impossible to market time effectively without one.

Actually, I do have a crystal ball

It sits on my desk. I gleefully push it in front of a client when asked what kind of return he or she will expect with their investment. Take a look! See anything? The ball came as a present from a gifted colleague of mine, who similarly loved a well-played joke. We are always told past performance is no guarantee of future performance, and anyone that guarantees returns on individual equity stocks is either lying or has attached an insurance policy to cover risk and has charged you a premium for it. I take joy in watching their faces as I push the ball in front of them as they start to realize I am pulling their leg by telling them I actually have a crystal ball. However, this one doesn't work very well.

Far too many investors choose their funds by only looking in the rearview mirror. They expect the same return as in the near past of the stock or mutual fund performance. Often they find the results for their portfolio the following year lacking luster as the market happens to move in reverse to their expectation. Clearly, the rearview-mirror method does not work well. Past performance is no guarantee of future results.

It is my belief the main purpose of a financial advisor is to handle the risk side of investment and to ensure the risk taken in a portfolio is appropriate to the client's life situation while managing their expectation. This is why communication is so very important in financial services. Documentation has become increasingly more important as disgruntled clients seek recourse through litigation for negligent behavior from their advisor. Suck it up; more signatures are required. The client's wish must be discussed and proven through documentation.

You need to join AA

Actually, I'm playing on words, or abbreviations to be more precise. I'm talking asset allocation, or the proportions of your portfolio allocated to stocks, bonds, and cash. Not Alcoholics Anonymous, unless that is your problem. Asset allocation is the best tool you have to ensure your portfolio is proper for your situation. Looking back, you will see a fifty-year history of stocks outperforming bonds by a wide margin but with much higher volatility. Bonds are generally used for injecting a smoother overall movement in growth but at a lower long-run rate of return.

Your financial situation is based on many factors, such as life cycle, income, age expectancy, dependents, as well as many particular financial projects or goals that you might have, such as funding your child's education or buying a car or cottage. It is said that asset allocation is one of the largest factors affecting your ultimate destination, although I might argue that starting early or staying invested may have a much larger effect on your total result.

Many books are written on the finer points of investing, but this is not my intention

My intention is to act as a catalyst to your excitement. Excitement for the real opportunity you have to improve your financial future. I would love to talk about my financial hero here, but trust me, you will hear about him soon enough.

Far too many critics sit on the sidelines, eager to criticize or reluctant to take educated guesses. Coulda, woulda, shoulda! As you will see later in the book, successful investment requires capital at some kind of risk. If there were such a thing as a risk-free investment having a guarantee of a large return, all investment would eventually migrate there. However, with increased risk comes increased potential return or loss. If it were not so, no one would ever take the higher-risk investment. It is my hope that your excitement will build not in the time it takes to read this material but over your lifetime as you track your personal results and realize the power of ownership.

If you already know it all, stop right here and drop the book back on the shelf

Part of the reason I feel compelled to place these thoughts on paper is the relative financial success I have enjoyed. This stuff has worked for me. I would rather have the wallet than the badge. What about you?

ROLF ELIASON

In two years of studying general science in the University of Alberta back in the midseventies, it was impressed upon me that curiosity is a vital component for advancement in knowledge. Observe. Awaken curiosity. Ask the questions how or why. Create a hypothesis to explain the observed phenomena and then throw absolutely anything against the hypothesis to prove it wrong. If you find anything that proves otherwise, stay with the hypothesis until you do. This is essentially the scientific method, which advances the discovery of truth. Answering curiosity is what science is all about, in my opinion.

While reading this book, you just may be surprised with a truth you haven't thought of before. Don't forget your curiosity. There is a huge difference between an atheist and an agnostic. The first one says, "I know there is no God." The latter of the two says, "I do not have enough information to really be sure." Oddly, the atheist seems to require more faith in his position than the agnostic. Okay, relax! My intention is to discuss my passion of financial advice, not to preach my faith.

If you are looking for simple, basic truth that may inspire you to take positive action, I believe this book is for you

Ever wondered why it is that success can happen to someone who was never even considered in a high school vote to be the most likely to succeed? I am always intrigued with material on the Internet showing stars with whom you may be familiar. They seem to be successful, beautiful, rich, you name it—and yet were ugly ducklings in high school. There has to be something in play that most are unaware of. But it definitely is in play. Just look at their results. Were they just plain lucky? Or did they just do something right? It seems to boil down to doing something right, getting lucky, or maybe a bit of both.

Ever notice the lucky guy?

When you talk about luck, there is no better place to direct your thoughts to than Las Vegas. The city of glitter and glitz! Yes, I have been there. I am not much of a card player, but I did know how to pull an arm on a slot machine. They have since replaced the side arm with a single button to push. Perhaps it takes less time to drop money into the machine using the button instead of the arm. Or possibly it might be to cater to laziness. Yes, I have also been the center of attention while sitting in front of one of these machines, although it was short-lived.

It was back in the days when the coins actually dropped into your bucket. There was a loud *ding-ding-ding* with each coin dropped, attracting even more attention. Nothing much else that can get your heart pumping more than running for more buckets to contain all the loot spewing out of your own machine. When is this going to stop spewing coins? I hope never! *Thump-thump, thump-thump!* Regretfully, I was not smart enough to fold and cash in. Are you kidding? I was on a roll! It did not take long for the buckets of coin to disappear back into the "one-arm bandit."

I have observed much of my early self when I have advised clients to take profits and sell a fund that has grown unusually fast and unusually high. They are very reluctant to sell the winner. It is just like the time at Las Vegas when I didn't have the smarts to fold when my buckets were full. What has ever happened to "buy low, sell high"? Emotion gets in the way. Ever notice the lucky guy? He just won a million dollars in the lottery. Ever notice the lucky guy? His slot machine is going *ding-ding-ding*.

Many people head to Vegas with more than just entertainment in mind. Somehow, in the back of their mind, they believe they are going to be that lucky one and win in a big fashion. Someone announces, "George, my friend's sister's brother-in-law, won a hundred grand last year." Uh-huh. Las Vegas has more often been referred to by some in a more practical way as Lost Wages.

However, for the majority of us, what is required is an appropriate strategy and implementation. It may take a lifetime. Most of us will never win that hundred grand. The odds are stacked against us. This is not even a book of business strategy so much as a book about my passion: personal finance planning and wealth accumulation.

Can you name the author of this quote: "Compound interest is one of the great wonders of the world"?

The author of this quote is from one of, if not *the* most, famous geniuses of modern times. He might be deemed the most famous that ever walked this earth. I am speaking of none other than Albert Einstein. Almost everyone is familiar with his formula that connects time, matter, and space: $E = mc^2$. Hey, the hydrogen bomb actually worked! However, those more familiar with quantum mechanics, the new paradigm of physics, would argue that Albert was wrong in another of his famous quotes: "God does not play dice." They might point to the fact that Niels Bohr, another famous physicist, coupled with the work of Werner Heisenberg, actually surpassed our beloved Albert on this one.

Nonetheless, it would not be hard to argue that Albert scored very high on his IQ test. And for Albert to be so taken with the power of compound interest and name it to be one of the great wonders of the world, there must indeed be something to it.

Some truths are very simple yet profound.

Why is it that some of the greatest truths we know are just plain and simple? Our friend Albert was at one point deemed simpleminded, if not deranged. Come on, he even flunked math! Maybe there is hope yet for me as Calculus 101 was never my strong point. Similarly, this book may seem frivolous or light reading, but I believe the contents can positively influence your financial life. These are not empty words. It worked for me. The power to change your future is between your ears. It is not just a question of your ability. It is not just a question of your aptitude either. It may boil down to an even bigger factor: *your attitude*. Next time you are hiring an employee or applying for a job yourself, think triple A. You just might score a triple-A employee or land the job yourself with these three attributes: ability, aptitude, and attitude.

Over the years I have observed salespeople who are very capable. There is no question they are fully able to do what is necessary to get the job done. They even have an impressive resume outlining their accomplishments. But their heart is elsewhere. *"I would rather be sailing!"* their bumper sticker would read. In my early years I was actually looking for a bumper sticker that would read, *"I would rather be selling!"* What is the difference? This is where I believe the second attribute comes in—their aptitude, or how they are cut. It is somewhere in their chromosomes. These people seem to be born that way.

It has also been my observation that certain salespeople are both able and seem to have the aptitude for their job. However, these capable, naturally inclined salespeople at times have one factor holding their performance back in a big way. Their attitude sucked. They hated either their boss, their job, or something else. Attitude boils down to how you present yourself when things aren't going your way. See what I mean about triple A?

I always believed my job as a salesman was to convince people that what I was proposing was in their best interest. Their benefits outweighed the costs. I had advantages and features to prove it. I believe this is the reason I am writing this book.

Can you name the author of this quote: "Compound interest within a tax shelter is even more wonderful than compound interest on its own. Best of all is compound interest that is tax free!"?

This quote comes from a financial advisor that knows how to legally avoid and defer taxes or convert income into tax-favored instruments, such as capital gains or dividends. We are talking legal tax avoidance here, not tax evasion. Tax evasion will land you in jail. Avoidance means using every legal means to prevent that "Viking pillaging and plundering" to which we feel victim at tax time. God bless our chartered accountants!

One of the best recent gifts from our government is the opportunity to save in a vehicle that does not tax you on interest, not ever! Interest, dividends, or capital gains remain tax-free within that vehicle: the tax-free savings account. It is often referred to with an acronym, TFSAs. Tax-free savings accounts are not to be confused as bank accounts having full liquidity, as there are definite rules attached to replacing withdrawals. Naturally, the government does not believe in simplicity. This advisor does not feel worthy of being even mentioned in the same chapter as Mr. Einstein but remarks, "Mr. Einstein did not live in an environment of 46 percent marginal tax grabs." Obviously, there is more at work here than compound interest.

Hmmm, most interesting . . .

Chapter Two

THE WIZARD OF CAUSE

A parable

Once upon a time, in a faraway land lived a man named Ozzie Causey and his family. Life was relatively good. He was well on this way to achieving goals that Ozzie had set for himself. He had completed high school, and although he wasn't voted most likely to succeed, his grades were good enough to land him in the university of his choice.

Ozzie worked diligently, and his grades were respectable. He was not a drifter; he knew what he wanted, and life was unfolding just the way he planned. With all his planning, life was about to get better.

Education was quite important to him as he knew he would never land that all-important job downtown without it. His job interview went well, and soon he was bringing home a fat paycheck that gave him license to adequately cover his needs. More importantly, he actually enjoyed his work.

That special gal he had his eye on was soon noticing that brand-new sports car in which he was jetting around town, and she happily accepted the invitations he gave her to attend theater, movies, sports functions, and the like. How could life get any better?

Life gets better

It wasn't long before the question was popped, and out popped the ring. "It's gorgeous!" she declared.

"So are you!" he retorted.

With that, Ozzie Causey scored. Soon they were married.

Before long they were able to prearrange a mortgage at the bank, and the two of them marched down the street with the real estate agent to view a home she had seen in the paper. "It's just perfect!" they declared. Papers were signed, sealed, and accepted. Congratulations to the new homeowners!

The next day the truck arrived with their belongings, and with a bit of effort, boxes were emptied and belongings designated to their proper location. "Mmm . . . what's that smell? Honey, I didn't know you knew how to bake apple pie!" He lit a fire in the fireplace. He lit another fire. But we aren't going there . . .

Nine months later, the joy of their lives arrived times two. Twins! Beanie and Cecil soon stole their hearts and fit well into the family. The parents faced the doo-doo generated; it was small and didn't smell bad, and they knew how to handle it. They wondered if it's true that when the twins grew to be teenagers, the doo-doo generated would be of a different kind. It just might be bigger and smell worse! *Would they know how to handle it?* One step at a time—Ozzie rolled up his sleeves and didn't mind one bit. Well, just a teeny bit . . .

Just at the point when life couldn't get better

Later that year, he arrived at work and was beckoned to his employer's office. "Causey?" bellowed his boss. "Yes, Mr. Grapple?" answered Ozzie timidly. "I have some very bad news. Our Grapple grommets have just been denied for the War Chester Shire job! It seems our grommets aren't grabbing the watch-a-ma-collets the way they are supposed to. Do you know what this means!"

Mr. Grapple continued his diatribe, barely coming up for air. "I can't stress enough how much that account means to this company! What other account is next: the Moose Tard Corporation? What about the Catch Up Foundation? Causey? You had better get on it—RIGHT NOW!"

Ozzie Causey winced. He knew how serious this was. Never in their entire history since George Grapple the First founded the company had Grapple grommets even come close to not adhering to the watch-a-ma-collets! Mr. Grapple the Third would not live up to his father's pride or his grandfather's. Losing the War Chester Shire account could end the company in Varsol. That is to say, in solvent, see? Ozzie suggested that he would work on it that night.

Mrs. Causey had no idea. Ozzie only told her he was working on a special project. The best he could come up with was to stretch the truth, or at least stretch the grommet. He came up with a plan.

The next day Ozzie went straight to Mr. Grapple's office. In a matter-of-fact manner, he cut right to the chase: "I'm sure if we stretch these grommets before sending them out, it will improve their e-last-icity. That is to say, their *e* component will outlast any grommets on the market. And by stretching them, my research shows they will become softer with a lower durometer. This means they will be softer than any other grommet on the market. Only then will they adhere to the watch-a-ma-collets. The problem is, ours have been too hard all along."

"Dammit, I like that!" exclaimed Mr. Grapple. "We'll stretch out our process right away!" Ozzie went home that night, relieved but still unsettled. He hadn't spoken loud enough to convince himself.

Two weeks later, the batch of one hundred thousand Grapple grommets were stretched and completed. Management at the watch-a-ma-collets factory were nearing their just-in-time set point. The durometer was checked. Yes, they were softer than any produced before. Now, the real test: Would they adhere to the watch-a-ma-collets? The batch was sent out for testing at the Tack-E testing lab.

Ozzie went home that night, feeling a little uneasy. What if the durometer had no bearing on adherence? Something has to make it stick! At least the story needed to stick, if not the grommet. What if . . . ? He didn't sleep well that night.

Of grommets and grimace

"Causey, get your ass down here!" bellowed Mr. Grapple. "These grommets don't stick worth a shit! Not only do they not adhere to watch-a-ma-collets, they don't stick *to* shit! And I doubt they would even stick to *your* shit either! YOU ARE FIRED!"

Suddenly, Ozzie Causey's life turned upside down. How will I pay the mortgage? How will I buy gas for the sports car? How will I buy food for my kids? How will I face Mrs. Causey? It was the last one that really troubled him. He headed home to face the music.

Actually, he walked. He thought he might clear his mind and emotions by walking. He would collect his thoughts on how to break the news. He stopped in to the Cheers-R-Us pub to see if his buddies were there and maybe cry in his brew. Like always, they were there.

Each of his buddies had his own ideas and ways of consoling poor Ozzie. But nothing changed the fact that he needed income to cover his continuing expenses. He thought of Beanie and Cecil. His eyes started to cloud as he returned to the journey home. Just as he turned the corner, he tripped.

Here's where the parable gets stretched a bit

He was going down a lane he had not traveled before. Turning the corner, he tripped over something and fell. "What? Surely I only had a couple of brew!" he muttered. He saw the culprit: a bottle that looked vaguely familiar. He brushed himself off and rubbed some mud off the label to see that the bottle actually came from the watch-a-ma-collets factory. He started to read the label, but before he could finish . . .

You guessed it, out pops the wizard

"Rough day?" asked the wizard with a wry smile.

"You have no idea," replied Ozzie.

"Oh, I know all about it," the wizard said. "Thanks for rubbing the bottle. I've been waiting over two hundred years since the last time I got out. Two hundred years is a heck of a long time in a place called Cause, and I couldn't wait to get out of that stupid place. It kind of gets a bit cramped in there in Cause Land." The wizard stretched his arms and yawned a bit. *"Just call me the Wizard—the Wizard of Cause.* So what's your wish?"

"Wait a minute, did you say 'Causey'?" asked Ozzie Causey.

"Nope," replied the wizard. "It is just Cause."

Ozzie Causey was confused. "Just Cause? Why would they give a place a name like that?"

"Why would your mother give you a name like Ozzie when your last name is Causey?" replied the wizard with another question.

"Just because!" said Ozzie.

Now the wizard was confused. The confusion settled into silence. Ozzie paused for a moment, thinking about his sudden fortune. After thinking a while longer, he asked the wizard, "Any wish at all?"

The wizard replied, "You got it, but only one. So make it a good one."

Ozzie thought of his family. He thought of his buddies. He thought of all the financial obligations that he was presently facing, and would be certain to face in the future. This wish had to be good.

"I don't want stuff. I mean, at least not now. The stuff will come. I am more interested in capacity to generate income—more income than I consume. Here is my wish: *I want to ask for the ability to generate enough income to service my needs and teach my buddies, I mean the friends and people I come into contact with, how to do the same."*

"Can't you count?" asked the wizard. "That's two wishes, not one! However, I am totally surprised by your request. I haven't in three thousand years seen anyone make a request like that! They usually ask for stuff like fancy yachts, mansions, the latest model of chariot, or even a fat bank account. Stuff to make them cool, and their friends start to drool. You know, they are concerned mostly about their image. When I grant those kinds of wishes, those guys usually end up bankrupt in a few years. It is easy come, easy go. Many people that win the lottery fare much the same. They know nothing about how wealth really works. They really don't know how to handle money either. They have no concern whatsoever to live within their means. It is just like I said, they want to be cool and make their friends drool."

Then the wizard recounted, "I once had someone actually get smart a thousand years ago, and he asked for a goose that laid a golden egg each day, but only one golden egg per day. Boy, did that work out well for him! Well, at least until one day he got a hankering for some stew and killed the goose. What an idiot! But I am surprised at you. What a smart request! This is about income, not stuff! I'll tell you what I'm going to do. You asked not only for the ability to generate income, but you thought about your family *and your buddies as well!* You are going to get both wishes!" The wizard shook hands with Ozzie, looking at him with pride, but quickly that fatherlike smile turned to one of impatient agitation. "Sorry, but the Big Guy is calling—I gotta go! Have a nice life!" *Poof!* And quicker than you can say 649, the wizard vanished, never to be seen again.

The denouement . . .

As you may well have guessed, Ozzie Causey spent the rest of his life in relative success. However, *success* is a relative word. His happiness was not generated by his sports car or even the home they bought, although they certainly were a source of enjoyment.

He recognized his real source of joy was family, being the best at what he purposed to do, leaving footprints in the sand, teaching his buddies how to generate enough income to meet their needs, enjoying the trip called life, and preparing for when the Big Guy eventually calls.

And they lived happily ever after.

The End

Well, that is the end of the parable but not the chapter. I think you likely get the gist of what I was trying to convey, but without wrecking the allegory, I would like to make a few comments.

As I mentioned in chapter 1, it is not my intention to write a deep, strategy-filled book on the finer points of investment. There are plenty of them out there. I have learned in life to focus on that last A: attitude. It probably would surprise the daylights out of my high school English teacher that forty years later I would write a book. That is, if he is still alive! I also mentioned in the previous chapter that I have stories that, if not told, will soon explode.

Having spent many years in sales, I have dealt with many people with many emotions. I love to be where the action is. I love the phrase "Git 'er dun."

You may have already guessed it. In the story I am Ozzie Causey. I consider myself one very fortunate man. Not because I tripped over a bottle, but I was related to the Wizard of Cause, my late father-in-law.

Writing this chapter, I chose the title with a great deal of thought and fond memories of how he handled both family and finance. Having spent most of his career in sales, sales management, and marketing, his no-nonsense approach often morphed into an intimidating stance. When I first met the man, I was intimidated by him. Back then he wore the Dick Tracy kind of business hat, a trench coat, and the cigar to boot. As the years wore on, intimidation melted into deep respect. I think he mellowed too.

Oh yes, he left footprints in the sand. And I know he enjoyed the sixty-nine years he was allotted. He always said the way he wanted to go was to be shot in bed by a jealous husband when he was ninety-three! I know he was joking. But he didn't make it to ninety-three.

What was his favorite song? Once again, I know he was joking: "Dropkick Me Jesus (Through the Goalposts of Life)"! Although we as family joked we would sing this at the service of celebration of his life, we recanted. Besides, Bill didn't make a field goal. *He scored with a touchdown.*

The day I asked the Wizard of Cause for the hand of his daughter in marriage, he didn't budge an inch from the carpet where he lay facedown, nor did he open his eyes. He just asked, "Can you support a wife and family?"

I think he liked my reply: "I can take care of her, but the rest of you are going to have to fend for yourselves!"

The last time I spoke with Bill at his home, I sensed his life's end was close, if not imminent. The cancer he fought so valiantly was getting the best of him. I thank God I had the opportunity to thank him. Many people do not get that opportunity because of circumstance. I told him the two most fortunate things of my life were marrying his daughter and his having the faith in me to take care of his friends and family in the same capacity as a financial advisor.

Bill was a wealth of information, but it was never given in a lecture. It was always tidbits here, tidbits there. He will always be revered and never forgotten.

How many of you have tripped over a bottle, and without warning, out jumps a Wizard of Cause?

Chapter Three

What Are You Doing with Your Life?

My story

I already know this chapter is not going to be one of my favorites. Maybe not yours either. However, I need to talk a little bit about myself and how I got here. I hope I don't bore you. If you can hold your nose through this chapter, there are tidbits to glean. Good ones, I believe.

Calculus for dummies

I have a confession to make. Calculus, a higher level of mathematics, has never been one of my stronger achievements. It is conventionally thought that it was Sir Isaac Newton who first bestowed calculus upon us. However, there is controversy. There are others who believe a man named Leibniz was working with it years before Newton. Regardless, I wish they had written *Calculus for Dummies* back in the late seventies while I was in engineering school. I could certainly have used the book back then.

My ability in calculus was pitiful, let alone challenged. Aptitude was likely the culprit. Check on attitude? Effort: yes, results: no. Clearly, partial differential equations and complicated trigonometry were not destined to be in my future. However, no education is ever a waste.

The university I attended retains its status and reputation. Just read the yearly Maclean's University ratings issue. It remains tough for students to get in. Mid-to-high-eighties high school marks are yet required, courtesy of supply and demand for the placements. I still recall the first open session of my engineering class. That would be over thirty-five years ago. I was sitting in a lecture theater and was seated along with a couple hundred other students. A professor was marching back and forth, barking at us like a sergeant, and telling us how fortunate we were to be there. "Take a look to the guy on your left. Take a look on your right. Only one of you will make it through fourth year." Unfortunately, I chose the wrong guys to sit beside.

From engineering to sales

Have you ever owned one of those wind-'em-up furry toy mice that scoot across the floor? Whenever they hit something solid, they automatically back up a bit, quickly turn, and head in a different direction. That's the story of my life. The direction of my career quickly turned to the field of industrial sales, a good place to cut your teeth, learning social skills. It was there I gained years of exposure to multilevel interaction with plant maintenance, purchasing, engineering, and senior management. At each level they would have their particular agenda, concerns, and hot buttons to push. A sales career for me was fun. Many salespeople are fairly opinionated, and I was no exception.

Ever notice how something said in a moment may stick with you forever?

Often there are little quips or sayings you come across in life that are never easily forgotten. Can you think of any? I think this is the essence of nursery rhymes taught in primary school grades and, perhaps as well, little songs taught to children in Sunday school. These jingles have catchy tunes, are difficult to forget, and carry important truth. My mother was of Norwegian descent and used to bounce me on her knees, teaching me songs in that native language—something about a little girl named Clara spinning wool. I wish Mom had instead taught me as a teenager a song about little girls spinning lies! That would have been of a bit more use. I digress.

There also seem to be words or sentences that we hang on to and are never forgotten. Time passes, and the words are often recalled, often quoted. I remember one of these quips came to me in the early eighties while watching Lady Diana Spencer speaking of her forthcoming marriage: "It's what I want!" Perhaps it was her thick English accent that made it so memorable.

Who can forget the words spoken by the late Neil Armstrong as he first stepped foot on the moon? "This is one small step for a man, one giant leap for mankind." How about the words proclaimed by Martin Luther King: "I have a dream!" Or the most famous retort spoken by Richard Nixon: "I am not a crook!" Who will ever forget the words of—or more specifically the way it was said by—the Gipper, Ronald Reagan: "Well, Nancy . . ."? Again, these words were spoken so powerfully and distinctly they are never forgotten.

From jazz to father-like advice

The title of this chapter in the book is chosen from one of my most unforgettable moments while seated in my own living room after dinner. One of those all-out kinds of meals that take hours to prepare. One of my favorite sayings to invited guests when they come to dinner is "I'm so glad you came for dinner. Now we will get something good to eat!" In case you're not quite sure, I would be pulling your leg, so to speak. I'm not sure if I said that to the in-laws when they came, but this meal was a quaint foursome meal—a daughter, her parents, and a son-in-law.

The big question

I enjoy playing jazz piano at a novice level, and after dinner I retired to the piano in the living room to start one of my favorite songs. Out of the blue a booming voice came across the room: *"What are you doing with your life?"* I instantly knew this was destined to be one of those unforgettable moments.

Was I startled? Yes, more than a bit. Such a bold, focused, chutzpah-filled, prying statement—my hands fell away from the keyboard, and I knew immediately the statement came from my own father-in-law, William Hopkins. I answered with a brief inventory of my life: industrial sales, a mortgage, feeding a wife with two kids. Maybe I better rephrase that: feeding a wife *and* two kids. It didn't take him long to summarize his future plans and how they would eventually affect me.

People/talk/money

He quickly gave his own assessment of his son-in-law at the piano, pointing out (1) "You like people," (2) "You like to talk. *Perhaps too much!*" he added, and (3) "You have a significant interest in the mutual fund industry." There was reason for all this chutzpah—he was on a mission. We'll discover more on that later. But first, let's discover more of his assessment. He was right on all three counts. One Thanksgiving dinner I was chatting up why a certain fund manager of a fund I owned had a 30 percent cash component. I also wondered aloud why this fund manager wasn't managing the whole pool of capital properly. Darned right I was interested in the mutual fund industry! At that point in my life, I was making as much in the stock market as the income I was making in my job in sales. And that is exciting, to say the least. Bill was, all the while, taking note of my interest. It certainly was building.

Have you not heard about DINKS: double income, with no kids? When my wife and I were first married, both of us were working outside the home, so we qualified. As we began to save our income, bit by bit we progressed toward becoming TRINKS: triple income, with no kids. Wait a minute! Two sons came along, so now the acronym didn't fit! Change it to TRICKS: triple income, complete with kids. If we could pony up income from another source, we would progress to QUICKS: quadruple income, complete with kids. *Now we're starting to dream.* I can hardly wait to get to chapter 4. We'll talk more about income there.

A simple but concise assessment

Bill had spent most of his life in sales and sales management within the plastics industry. The last seven years of his life were spent in financial advice, a vocation not only of which he was capable but he was actually cut for it. For him, providing financial advice was a hobby. Yes, he knew how to hustle in new business and bring in lots of new clients, but that was not his desire. His desire was to financially plan specifically for friends, family, and himself too, of course. To him this wasn't work; he enjoyed doing it. He certainly didn't *need* the work. Bill's attitude toward his work was impeccable as well. Triple A, like we discussed. But unknown to us, Bill was working on a secret mission. It was a mission of transition.

Another fork in the road ahead

At the piano, I knew from the tone in his voice there was some kind of plan he had in mind. It had taken me nearly twenty years to work myself into the level of competence I achieved in technical sales. For the most part I was happy in what I was doing. But this was going to be life altering. This was a Neil Armstrong moment. To the moon and back! It takes a special person that easily accommodates change. I am not that special. This was a giant leap for me, not a step.

I have a question for you. I know it is far-fetched, but there's allegory here. If Neil's father had been waiting on the moon, ready to help Neil off the ladder, do you think Neil would have taken his hand? I think you know the answer.

The plan

After his three-point summary of my character, he then laid out his carefully thought-out plan:

- I would start taking Internet courses during the evening on financial planning, all the while maintaining my industrial sales job and not disrupting family income.

- Once I achieved a certain level in financial education, I would then submit a letter of resignation to my industrial sales employer and join my father-in-law in the business of financial advice.

- He would then work me as a copartner into the list of clients he had developed, training me not only in client relations but the business end of it as well. The learning curve would be steep.

- Once I achieved a certain level of confidence, he would then bow out, and I would be up and running.

Sometimes life delivers a big surprise

Let's cut to the chase. It didn't take much deliberation. I started the evening Internet courses, all the while attending to my duties in sales. Everything according to *the plan*. Eventually I started completing courses, and everything was going according to schedule until an unexpected fax arrived in my home office on Halloween Day, 1998. A book of business had come up for sale from the surviving spouse of a financial advisor. The advisor had suddenly passed away. The spouse approached Bill, asking him to purchase her husband's book of business. Bill accepted but only on the condition of my decision to change course. Suddenly the plan was on the fast track.

His urgent suggestion came quickly to me: "It's now or never. Quit your job!" Two weeks later, Bill and I signed the purchase agreement drafted by the lawyer, and after giving the required notice, I was out of a job. That night, I was out for a coffee with a close friend, announcing my new business venture and asking for his advice. I was seasoned enough to realize that outside eyes (especially eyes from someone who knows me well) could give me insight to which I might be blind. I was fully aware of my own opinion; I was searching for truth.

However, that night I came home and found my wife in a very upset state. This was yet another unforgettable moment. "Dad is under the knife for surgery. It's some kind of internal blockage." Indeed, 1999 was going to be an unforgettable year.

Was this a big surprise? Yes. More than that, it was a huge shock. It turned out to be non-Hodgkin lymphoma, and the next nine-month period for our whole family was straight from hell. My father-in-law, who was friend, mentor, and financial hero, was battling cancer in a losing fashion. All the while I faced a steep learning curve of both client situation and the business of financial service. Indeed, 1999 was unforgettable.

My wife, her family, and I were present with Bill when he eventually passed away. No, it wasn't easy. This was one of the most poignant moments of my life. Why am I sharing so much personal family information? Well, all our parents are now deceased, and I doubt they would care much. Financial advice involves estate planning, which certainly is personal. It also involves facing hard and cold facts. I said to my wife after the death of our fourth parent, "I guess this means we're next up to bat."

It is personal

The business of financial advice deals with wealth accumulation. It deals as well with wealth management and wealth distribution either while you are alive or upon the death of the testator. Many people disdain discussing their own mortality. An ostrich, when faced with danger, loves to stick his head in the sand. If it is out of sight, it is not there, right? Wrong! Don't be an ostrich. Concerning mortality, certain important details, such as your last will and testament or life insurance, need to be dealt with and not ignored.

When I hear statistics that today only 50 percent of Canadians have in place a properly prepared last will and testament, it sickens me. Either you can decide the destination of your hard-earned estate or the government will decide how it is distributed for you. That may or may not be to your satisfaction, particularly for those in a second or third marriage. Take your pick, but my advice is to go see your lawyer. Your estate reflects a lifetime of your work. The government has cherry-picked off you all your life. Don't let them decide about the remainder. Look up the word *escheat* in the dictionary or Google it. This is scary stuff.

ROLF ELIASON

Take it from the wizard

Let me back up to my financial hero. There were several points in my life where his fatherlike advice stuck like glue. One of those moments came when he came close into my personal space, looking me straight in the eye, and out came his booming voice again, saying, "Rolf, do you want to become a wealthy man?"

I didn't bat an eye and quickly replied, "Sure, lay it on me!"

He then said, "Get this one word emblazoned on the back of your brain: *ownership*. Only ownership gives you legal rights to both capital gains and dividends, which can never be taken from you. Not without severe gymnastics in the House of Commons. And dividends and capital gains are tax favored. If you go into *loanership*, you approach the banker's desk and humbly ask what he will give you for the utility of the money you are handing over. The banker is now in the driver seat, deciding for you what interest rate you will get.

"Here is the crunch. The banker quotes a very low interest rate and says to get a better rate, you have to leave it locked in for a while. He may not have even mentioned inflation or taxation. As well, the interest income is fully taxed at your marginal rate. *Loanership* is for losers!"

Well, not quite exactly so, Bill. Obviously my father-in-law was a strong believer in ownership. He passed away in the fall of 1999, well before the tech stock bubble bursting in 2002 and missing the subsequent movement of the TSX and S&P 500. He did not see the second worst year in 187 years in the history of the Toronto stock market exchange. The worst occurred during the time of the Great Depression. I muse to myself in wonderment whether he would be exposed to the same proportion of stock if he had gone through 2002 and 2008. Probably not! It's been a different world of investment out there since 1999. *Different in some ways.*

Oh, to be twenty-five again!

When I was about twenty-five years old and not yet married to his daughter, Bill approached me to pass on his views. I had just started full-time employment in sales. Oh, he had chutzpah back then as well. This moment turned out to be the best piece of financial advice I have ever been given. He was encouraging me to put 10 percent of my earnings into savings. "Come on, Bill, get real. I want to buy a truck, not save for forty years from now! I'm only twenty-five years old. And you say 10 percent of my income? I certainly can't afford that."

He then spoke words that have stuck with me for life: "You start now, and when you are in your fifties, you will be thanking me. Compound interest is just that powerful. If you can't start with 10 percent, start with 5 percent and work your way up. Get excited about saving, Rolf, because savings is how wealth is accumulated."

Well, thank you, Bill. I know you're up in the clouds somewhere, but thank you.

Fishing lessons, not the fish

There are many other fundamental lessons he taught by word and example. Saving was an important one, but so was starting early. Here is another one. During the time he was enduring chemotherapy in 1999, he said one day to me, "You are not perfect, and neither is anyone else. What you really need to do is source out professionals in the area where you are lacking and utilize their service."

Wow. Am I one lucky guy or not? Tidbits here and tidbits there, but they aren't really tidbits. These were the full cow! How could it be that I would end up with all these pieces of valuable advice that, if followed, would bode for me in a way I had no comprehension? Their value certainly was not fully understood until years later.

I have heard it said, "Give a fish to a man and he will eat for a day. Teach him to fish and he will eat for a lifetime." Thank you, Bill, again. I love fishing.

Everyone needs a hero or two

It is my guess you have heard enough about me and possibly members of my family as well. It is kind of like getting stuck on a plane next to a proud, loud grandparent, complete with a full picture album and dozens of stories. Yikes! But first, let me tell you of one more of my financial heroes, the late Mr. Paul Rockel, founder of a pioneering mutual fund company, Regal Capital Planners Ltd. He passed away in December 2012.

I first heard Mr. Rockel speaking at a financial seminar sponsored by my father-in-law along with another financial advisor in the local area. One of those "fill 'em up with goodies and coffee and tell 'em a story" types of seminars. I yet recall what he said that night. His message was for me an "I have a dream" kind of moment: true, powerful, and unforgettable.

Here is the message he gave that night, and I am paraphrasing it in bullet form:

- There are two ways on this earth to make money:
    - Person at work.
    - Money at work.
- How to get money at work?
    - Person at work receives a wage.
    - Person lives within their means.
    - Person puts the extra money into an investment and leaves it there.
- Person lets the power of compounding work for them.
- Person makes sure it goes into a vehicle that has asset allocation appropriate to their life situation.

- Person makes sure it goes into a vehicle that is tax sheltered.

- Do not disturb!

Can you not see why this man has become a hero to me? It is simple. It works. And it worked for me. He is my financial hero number 2. As I stated earlier, some of the greatest truths are just that: simple and true.

If you want to buy, buy. If you don't, no touch!

I absolutely love Prince Edward Island. Our family has a history of getting outdoors with our beloved pop-up Coleman camper trailer. One of our trips to PEI was when our boys were around ten and eight years old. They were mulling about in a shops in Cavendish when they were confronted by the shop owner. In the car, all the way back home to Ontario, the boys were forever emulating the ethnic accent of a command given to them by the shop owner: "EEF YOU VANT TO BUY, BUY. BUT EEF YOU DON'T—NO TOUCH!"

This was another one of those unforgettable-truth moments. This is a slogan never forgotten, at least not in our family. Please give me the freedom to adjust it to fit our purpose just a bit. Mutual funds are designed for long-term use. They are not designed for trading in and out of with market movements. Registered Retirement Savings Plans may be used in financial emergencies but again are designed for retirement use. Do not touch your savings. Not until your feet are up in retirement. End of story.

A little bit about hockey success

There are likely hundreds of thousands, if not millions, of hockey fans that point to Wayne Gretzky as their hero and point to his title as the Great One. He deserves the title as he knows the game inside out. Here is one of the messages that he gave during a sports interview. I believe it was after one of his many successful games on the ice. When asked about the secret of his success in scoring so many goals on ice, his answer to the sports reporter was priceless. This has been quoted by many people in the financial industry and rightly so. He said, "Many players chase the puck. I skate to where I know the puck is going."

Wow! Is that not applicable to investment or what? Many investors are indeed out there chasing results and not adjusting their play to suit their particular life situation, all the while not even using a best guess of economic activity. Many just chase last year's winners. Some roll the dice. Worse yet, others get discouraged, throw up their hands, take their skates off, and vow never to get back on the ice again. Those that sold off equities after the fall of prices in 2008 lost out on strong positive results in 2009. It is not where the puck has been. It is where it is going. Thank you, Wayne.

An unfortunate mistake people make is in following their emotion. Skate to where the puck is going. Keep your skates on.

Regarding financial success

We will be discussing more of these issues in chapters that follow. Throughout this chapter I have discussed my life experience and the financial heroes that I have looked up to. It is my intention to write more about my passion. I am concerned regarding your financial future. Thank you for sitting next to me on the plane, along with my album and stories.

You have already met my wizard. Now that you have become acquainted, let's move on to the more important chapters.

Chapter Four

THE LAKE OF TWO RIVERS

You have heard of a keynote speaker. This would be my keynote chapter. I am quite excited to get these thoughts on paper. This is stuff that turns my crank.

For any parent, one of the greatest joys is watching your children grow to adulthood. We all aspire to see them grow into happy, productive people. As part of the God-designed life cycle, we also aspire to see little grandkids. They would be little bundles of joy that your children parent and raise. I have always been an advocate of focusing on the positive. Every parent has their own share of memories with their child. This was one of those many positive father-son moments I will never forget.

Like, how do you get rich? How do you make a lot of money?

The words came out of the blue, yet I understood them to be probable from my fifteen-year-old son. I had just resigned from my career as an industrial salesman, and he was fully aware of the direction I was heading. I knew this was going to be one of those moments not to be forgotten. I wanted what I was about to say to stick for a long time. I chose to tell a story.

"Those are two questions, Carl, not one. They are not the same question either. Making a lot of money and keeping a lot of money are two different issues. Do you remember the year my brother Don and I took a canoe trip in Algonquin Park?"

"Yes, but why didn't you take me?" he quipped.

"There wasn't much room in the canoe, and it was a brother thing. There is a lake in Algonquin Park we traveled called the Lake of Two Rivers. What do you think that means?" I asked. Carl was thinking.

River A and river B

"I guess there would be a river that fills the lake and another that drains the lake," he replied.

"That is a very good answer. Now, pretend you are a civil engineer. How would you make the lake grow?" I asked.

He thought for a moment and gave this answer. "I would get a big river going in. Then the lake would grow."

I could see he was listening closely and calculating. I then said, "That is not a bad answer, but it is not the correct one. That does not take into account the size of the river draining it." As an aside, many of the clients to whom I have told this story answer, "Dam the river going out of the lake. Then the lake will grow." Even that answer is not a bad answer, but it is not correct either.

Filling or draining

Following through, I then said to my son, "The correct answer must account for both the inflow and the outflow of the water. That is to say, the comparative volume rate flow of each river. The difference between these two factors will determine whether the lake will grow or shrink, depending on *which one is larger than the other*, the one filling the lake or the one draining it."

A must be greater than B

Carl was quick to get the point. That is to say, he understood the mechanics of water. He then reflected, "I think I get it. The river filling the lake has to be bigger than the one draining it. Then the excess water not drained by the flow out will accumulate in the lake. It makes total sense to me!"

I was proud and eager. I was proud of his assessment and most eager to get to the real point of my story. "Carl, I am not talking about civil engineering. I am talking about the answer to your two questions. You asked me about making a lot of money. You also asked me about becoming wealthy. I already told you these questions are not the same."

Income

I continued, "Today there many people with many differing levels of income. Their income includes income from all sources. Usually, the main source of income is their remuneration."

He quickly interrupted, "Remuneration? What's that? Dad, quit using big words."

I continued, "It is what the employer gives to you in return for the work you do, which may include things beyond just money. Some people are fortunate to have several sources of income. Possibly their spouse works outside the home as well receiving an income for the work he or she does. They may rent out part of their home, or possibly let someone use their cottage for a period in return for rent. They may even be paid royalties."

"What are royalties?" he asked, sitting, truly interested.

"Well, those songs you listen to on the radio . . . every time the radio plays a song, the radio station must pay a royalty or commission to the artist. It may not be much for each song played, but the individual payments all add up. Think of it. That song you like may be playing right now at a dozen radio stations across the country at this very moment.

And that relatively small royalty has now been multiplied by twelve. That is how the artist makes an income. Those royalties may even continue past the death of the artist, when it is paid to his or her estate."

"Wow! And you thought I wasted money on my electric guitar? What's an estate? Dad, cut the big lingo!"

"An estate is composed of things the artist owns when he dies. If he was smart, before he dies, the artist would have a lawyer express his wishes in a legal document called a last will and testament. This would be the artist's final wish to distribute what he owns to beneficiaries of his choice. That is, the part of his or her estate that is left and not yet taken by the government. No one knows their date of death (thank God for that one), so it is important that document gets drafted as soon as possible. The artist would name beneficiaries in the will. These are the people to whom he or she would want the estate to go in the event that he or she dies. As I have shown you, royalties are one of many sources of income."

"I can see you don't think much of the government," noted my son.

"Carl, my opinion is quite the contrary. In fact, they provide social services to people in need. Yes, there is abuse in the system, but there are people who have fallen through the cracks and have no other source of income to cover their needs. Not everyone is fortunate to have several sources of income. Some do not have even one income, and rely on these social services for their basic life needs."

Lifestyle

Having said enough on that, I decided to progress to the next item. "People also have differing levels of lifestyle. Lifestyle is the way they live, the car they drive, the home they live in, the clothes they wear, and the trips they take. The part that others see is the way they live. It is also like the frosting on the cake—the only part of the cake you actually see until it is cut. Lifestyle is all about image. This includes what they eat and whether they are eating at home or in a fancy restaurant. However, their wealth is something you really cannot judge without financial examination."

"Kind of like you telling me you can't judge a book by its cover?" he asked.

"That is exactly what I mean," I replied.

Wealth

"There is one more thing about your two questions. Being rich as you described concerns financial wealth, which is the part you would not see. Not too many people go around showing others their bank statement or lines of credit being used. Financial wealth is assessed correctly only when you look at the monetary value of all things owned and subtract the monetary value of all things you may owe, like mortgages, car loans, student loans, and the like."

Carl had not taken his eyes off me, so I knew this was of interest and he was following. I continued with my observation. "It is surprising, the number of people who do not disclose all to their financial advisor. We are not able to do our job properly without seeing the whole picture."

"What do you mean?" he asked.

"I can only guess they may be a little embarrassed about a loan they took out for whatever reason. Some do not even like disclosing how much money they make, or keep some sources of income hidden."

"Why would they do that?" he asked in disbelief.

I scratched my head and contorted my face for a bit of drama. "I am not exactly sure. These are the same people that do not shy away from a rubber glove on their doctor's hand!"

Carl was now getting impatient. "Dad, I get it. Move on."

"Let's get back to financial wealth. A financial advisor calls that net worth, which equals assets minus liabilities. In other words, things you own minus things you owe. That gives the advisor a snapshot of the client's finances at that moment in time. That is a good way to measure progress. That is what I think you were referring to when you asked me about getting rich, am I not correct?"

"I guess so." He still looked just a bit puzzled.

Hammering home the analogy

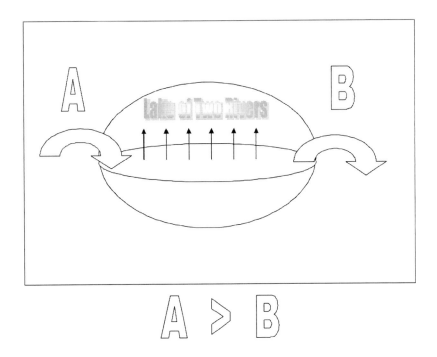

I then got to the meaning of the story. "Carl, here is the point: *the river into the lake is income. The river draining the lake is lifestyle. The Lake of Two Rivers in our story is wealth.*"

A light went on

Carl sat quietly for a moment, calculating. He then exclaimed, "I completely get it! If you want your wealth to grow, you have to ensure the total sources of your income exceed the cost of your lifestyle. Then your wealth will start to grow."

A smile grew upon one proud dad. I was confident the story would stick. Am I bragging about my son? Yes, I am.

I hope the story sticks with you, the reader, as well. Not so much when you are up in Algonquin Park, but when you are thinking about that next purchase and sorting out needs versus wants. Controlling your financial habits will have a dramatic effect on your wealth. It is my fundamental belief the heart of personal finance is living within your means.

Rome was not built in a day

Although these are basic, simple financial truths, many believe it to be more complicated than it really is. Rome was not built in a day, and unless you are a lottery winner or receive a large inheritance, I doubt your wealth will be either. When you are talking about the Lake of Two Rivers, the economics of the equation is the same. A must be bigger than B. The same thing is said by *"Live within your means."* The same is said by accountants when they speak of net savings.

This must be a focal point, or something

The same was stated so well by an author for whom I have a great deal of respect. I mean, how many heroes can a guy have? Without having you think, *Here we go again with his heroes*, I would like to talk briefly about one more: David Chilton. In financial circles, his book *The Wealthy Barber* is a must-read, as well as is his second, *The Wealthy Barber Returns*. Buy his books. Both these books are a wealth of information. There are few books, other than the Bible, that I can honestly say changed my life. David's book fit that category. Perhaps now you understand why I call him a hero.

I won his first book as a door prize around the time it was first published, and didn't then realize the effect that book would eventually have on me. His mantle of "Pay yourself first!" summarizes the principle of living within your means. It truly is the heart of financial planning. Mr. Chilton's insight had a direct effect upon my financial habits, which in turn influenced my decision to quit selling industrial equipment and start selling people on the idea of living within their means.

That's it? Yes, that's it.

It doesn't matter if you are making six figures of income per year or have a low-paying job. The equation remains the same. A must be bigger than B. Your total sources of income must exceed your total expenditures. If it doesn't, your wealth will not grow. Oh, you may have times in your life when your river size reverses temporarily, but if you want the lake to grow . . . I think you get the idea.

The economic truth applies whether you are talking about an individual, a group of individuals, a company, *or even a country*. You must live within your means or ultimately face the music.

Countries have a few alternatives that you or I have no access to. They can print money and devaluate their currency. They can reduce services or increase the level of taxation upon its citizens to improve their balance sheets. Worse yet, they can default on their debt. Yikes, that is the stuff that wars are made of. My battleship is bigger than yours, so what are you going to do about it?

Am I being simplistic? Maybe it is a bit shallow. I have already confessed that I am not a rocket scientist and have no aspirations for public office whatsoever. A bull in a china shop comes to mind. However, as a financial advisor, I am very concerned about public debt and watch very closely the direction our politicians head.

A very scary website I was once directed to is www.usdebtclock.org. Please take the time to go there, but go in trepidation. Here financial statistics are revealed concerning the state of our neighbors to the south, the United States of America. These calculations are constantly being updated and recalculated in live time. Canadian statistics are similarly shown but with less detail at www.debtclock.ca. A little knowledge is a dangerous thing, so they say. I should stick to the things I know and have done reasonably well with: simple and basic financial truths. And I do want you to continue reading to the end of the book.

I am concerned about public and private debt but remain fully invested. My concern is not so much for the near term of market movements, but I really wonder about marginal tax rates that will be needed to keep the system going twenty years hence. I am well aware of tax rates in countries from where my grandparents came, namely the Scandinavian countries. Their marginal tax rates are very high indeed, which is the cost of socialism, I might add. I am wondering if my sons will have similar marginal rates when they get to be my age. I hope not!

Have we baby boomers or our parents lived collectively within our means? Take a look at the website, and I think you will agree the answer is a definitive no. What kind of future do we wish to leave to our kids? I leave that to the politicians. With that, I will graciously bow out of this somewhat political discussion.

With that out of the way and off my chest, let's move on to some plain and simple truth.

Chapter Five

THE PLAIN, SIMPLE TRUTH

How do you eat an elephant?

"Come on! I'm spending time reading a book I fully anticipated to be on personal finance and hope to have some benefit in doing so! And this chapter, 'The Plain, Simple Truth,' starts with a joke?"

The years I spent in sales gave me many opportunities to observe people. There have been many occasions where I was guided through a plant to observe problems needing resolution. Knowledge of both product and customer situation is essential to turn product features into specific advantages. A seasoned sales representative knows how to focus on client concerns and how the product will benefit the customer. "What is in it *for me*?" the prospective customer is asking himself. For the astute salesperson, that is the hot button to push.

I was no exception, and while customizing a solution, I would draw the sale to a close, with a focus on benefits. I know I am splitting hairs here, but talking about a solution to the problem deals mostly with advantages of the product, not the benefits. It is emotion wrapped around "What's in it for me?" that truly sells. Only after hitting the hot button would I watch and wait. Watch for changes of facial expression or things said. Watch for any objection, and deal with it. I am not in front of you, watching your facial expression as you read this, but I suspect your patience is waning.

I have reason to start with a simple joke. "How do you eat an elephant?" has a very short punch line: *"One bite at a time."* It hits you with a bit of surprise. The punch line is short but also hits you with a moment of "A-hah!" You didn't really think about that, but it occurs to you: "Yes, that is true." That is what the plain, simple truth often does.

Most complex problems really are not that complicated if broken down into small components. This is a strategy taught in systems design engineering to systematically break the complication into specific components, which are more easily solved. They would not only be solved individually but collectively as well.

A white elephant nobody wants

Let's go back to the elephant. Let's call it a white elephant. How do you get rid of a white elephant? *How did that white elephant get here?* That changes focus, does it not?

Suddenly you realize something allegorical is being said. There is an implication of something that is difficult to get rid of and is overbearing. This is a cost-versus-benefit evaluation. It is not worth owning. It is also awkward and difficult to remove. Are we talking here about personal debt? Yes.

It is not quite the same as using the phrase "a white elephant in the room." Here the phrase is used to describe a situation that is either being ignored or not addressed. It remains uncomfortably big. It needs to be dealt with, but no one seems to step up to the plate to resolve it. A very good example is the person who is intestate and for whatever excuse refuses to get a last will and testament drafted or updated by a lawyer.

One bite at a time

How do you eat an elephant? One bite at a time! The action you take in a given moment does matter. However, I would argue there is something that matters more than that action you take. What matters more is your continued behavior. *What will you continue to do?*

Having a deluxe hamburger will not make you overweight. Unless the calories are burned off, eating a deluxe hamburger every night of the week likely would.

That same simple truth can be applied to personal finance. Whether or not you make an individual purchase will not likely throw you into bankruptcy. However, it could if you were on the brink of it. The patterns of financial behavior you develop dramatically affect your wealth either positively or negatively. Do not forget the "cool and drool" piece of advice from the Wizard of Cause. As well, the only way to eat the white elephant is one bite at a time. It is your continued financial habits that count, not your individual choice.

Look outside the box.

Continued lifestyle

You may save money on a particular purchase by buying it when it is on sale or save your money by not purchasing it at all. Obviously, the problem you were trying to solve by making the purchase would remain. If you passed on making the purchase, your capital would remain.

What you purchase matters to a sales manager, but what matters to him or her far more than your purchase is what causes you to keep coming back. What is in the back of his or her mind is "What can we do to ensure the buying cycle continues?" In the realm of your long-term finances, what is important is not so much the individual purchase or spending choice you make. It is *your collective choices that count.* Continued lifestyle matters greatly in the long run, regarding your personal finance. The question of what lifestyle will be correct for your personal financial situation is a question I cannot answer for you here. It depends on your sources of total income. Talk to your financial advisor. That is his or her expertise.

Swedish gasoline

Salespeople tend to drink a fair amount of coffee in a day. I know being a salesman really doesn't have anything to do with the choice, but most salespeople I know do and close many of their deals with a client over a relaxing cup of coffee. It was likely twenty-five years ago when I began taking an inventory of my consumption of coffee. Not the particular cup at the moment but my habit of drinking coffee.

I began to think about the amount of sugar and cream stirred into my cup. I began to think about my long-term consumption of sugar and cream. How much would I consume in a day, week, or over the year? I actually took out a calculator and started multiplying. I began to wonder about the long-term effect on my health. I began to shudder. Have you noticed how many sentences I have used starting with "I began"? I smell a change coming.

A change of habit and preference

It may have been the time I actually heard someone in the coffee line ask for "Quadruple sugar, quadruple cream." No, it wasn't me, but it spurred me into thinking about my own choices. Rather than a particular decision on a single cup of coffee, I made a rational choice of habit. I decided to pass on any cream or sugar in my coffee on a go-forward basis. It was strictly a health decision.

The taste did not sit right with me at first, but after a week or so, I became used to it. What about now? If I try the coffee the way I had been consuming it, now it does not seem to taste right with either the cream or sugar. This was a conscious reversal of habit leading to an actual change of taste.

Another change of habit and preference

I had another habit and, I might add, a good one—one that could be improved. Early in our married life and in the development of our own household portfolio of wealth accumulation, we were in the habit of saving. Our habit was to watch closely the level of income in our savings account at the bank, and whenever a couple of thousand dollars accumulated in the account, I then would make an appointment to go see our financial advisor. The meetings were productive, mostly dealing with wealth accumulation and learning. One by-product of these meetings was exposure to an area I had not yet fully understood: *the direction I would eventually be heading.*

Dollar cost averaging

Many of the fine books on personal finance speak of dollar cost averaging. Dollar cost averaging takes the guesswork out of timing and knowing when it is best to buy stocks or mutual funds. The process requires three components: a regular deposit, the same size of deposit, and an investment in the same stock or mutual fund.

Considering the volatility of the market and the fact that no one has a crystal ball that works to assist them in market timing, I believe there is very good reason to dollar-cost-average. Many argue dollar cost averaging removes guesswork on the best time to buy stocks. They note that more shares are obtained when purchased at a lower price per share.

Forced savings

My argument for dollar cost averaging focuses more on the aspect of forced savings, not market movements. Money out of sight is money out mind. It is out of the danger of squander. The funds are not stockpiled in your bank account, all the while waiting for the market to drop and then making your purchase.

Meanwhile, ideas keep cropping up of how else to utilize your capital saved. Have you ever noticed how fast the stock market can change? Old Quick Draw McGraw just popped back into my thinking. How fast are you on the draw? I have observed many people (including myself) whose attitude changes when unexpected capital comes their way. "Aw, let's take the trip. We can afford it! Aw, let's finish the basement. Aw, it's time to replace the car." It is at those points that careful reflection needs to take place. Is it a need, or is it a want? What is the total picture?

Deciding to change a habit

Similarly, like the conscious decision regarding sugar and cream, I went to my advisor and decided to change the way that I was saving. Instead of waiting for capital to accumulate in my savings account, with a danger of my attitude changing toward the capital saved, I would strategically get the money out of sight. For our family, saving for our future was nonnegotiable. It was set as an absolute imperative. I asked him to set up a preauthorized checking system: a PAC.

A preauthorized checking plan, PAC

This would automate savings and would be done without needing to meet with my advisor each time of purchase. In a PAC, the dealer is given authorization to take a set amount out of the banking account each month and automatically make a purchase into a fund choice set at the time the PAC was first set up. Changes to the investment, amount, or frequency could be adjusted as my situation changed. Apart from a decision of change, the investment would be made each month without thought and without bother. Automatically! This would not only be dollar cost averaging, it wouldn't "hurt" as much as writing that check for a couple of grand. This previous method of saving really stung back then. I had many other uses for that capital where it could otherwise be spent. To me, this new way of saving gave pain relief.

When is the best time to decide?

Some of you have decided to save for yourself this year, but deposit savings to your RRSP on an ad hoc basis. Perhaps you wait until February when you wait to see what is available and then decide how much you will contribute to your plan. I am suggesting that you make your decision based on your goal for the year, not on February leftovers. Automatically save month after month, year after year, and not wait. In February you may be like Old Mother Hubbard, who went to the cupboard, only to find the cupboard was bare.

Get automated in your savings, not ad hoc

My recommendation to clients is to go the automated route. Some people need to live by a strict budget, and through strict budgeting, pay close attention to where the money is going. In setting up the PAC, I applied the KISS principle to our own household. This was accomplished by deciding what I wanted us individually to save that year, dividing the number by twelve, and setting up a PAC for that amount with the dealer. This style of forced savings was found to be much simpler and much easier for us. It is simple, and it works well.

There is power in simplicity

This chapter is focused on plain, simple truth. Many of these lessons taught came from my heroes, but not all. And surely, not everything is as it first appears. Many people try to *reinvent the wheel*, so to speak. Where did this saying come from, and why was the wheel chosen as the example? The wheel is one of the most powerful tools invented by man. There is nothing simpler than round. Each point on the circumference is the same distance from one distinct point: the center. Why make it complicated? Why change it? If it is not broken, then do not fix it!

Personal finance, for the most part, is much the same. In many ways personal finance is basic common sense. However, in many cases common sense may only be partially understood and often not practiced. Or perhaps your opinion does not line up with the facts. Many of these principles regarding financial health need to be applied over long periods of time to get the full advantage of compounding. Some financial projects require fewer years to accomplish.

If your grandchild is headed for postsecondary education, you really should take advantage of the Canada Savings Education Grant the government offers. This program, since 1998, offers a 20 percent grant on contributions to a set limit per year. The grant is in the form of extra shares purchased based on purchases made to the plan. It also offers you the advantages of compounding growth and tax deferral. Ultimately the growth and grant are taxed in the hands of someone that usually has a lower marginal tax rate than you. It would be taxed in the hands of your grandchild.

However, this is where the simplicity starts to evaporate because the government is involved. Once again my purpose in this book is to excite you and focus on possibilities, so we will not explore that further. I am selling sizzle to you, not the steak. I want to focus on "What is in it for you?" and not specific features of mutual funds or financial vehicles.

Income minus expenditures: there is power in net savings

We have seen in the previous chapter that living within your means is one of the greatest financial sources of power there is. However, one must compare both income and expenditures to find these net savings.

Coming across a mentor early in life is a tremendous gift. A mentor who teaches by word, life, and example that savings is the real path to wealth. Is that simple, or what? Sadly there are many who just don't get it. Can you think of someone to whom you could become that Wizard of Cause? Do you love your family? Lead by example, and be sure to teach those lessons. You could be remembered for their lifetime for the gift of knowledge you gave. They may even write a book with you honorably mentioned in it.

There is power in compounding

We have read about some of the greatest people of all time: Warren Buffett, Wayne Gretzky, Albert Einstein, and Richard Nixon. Just kidding on the last one! You get my point. I can hardly believe Einstein failed math. Somehow, I just can't get my head around that. I am sure he studied the mathematics of money in order to call it one of the wonders of the world.

Future value equals present value multiplied by the sum of the rate of return plus one, which has been raised to the power of an exponent. This exponent is the number of compounding periods, and in the case of annual interest, the number of years you let it sit.

This exponent thus represents the time issue of money and is very, very powerful. No wonder my Wizard of Cause approached me when I was twenty-five.

There is power in observation, practicality, and change

Early in our family life we became aware of a story I think is worth noting. We heard of a family whose child went to a home for child care where housekeeping was, to say the least "needing attention." The child would continually come home with wet pants each time his mother picked him up from the home. His mother knew full well her son was potty-trained, and she asked him why he would not pee in the toilet during the time he was there. She never would have this problem with her son at home. What was the answer? Out of the mouth of babes, *"No, I can't! It is DIRTY!"*

The points taken here from this smart young man are observation, practicality, and change. You don't need to reinvent the wheel. You might need to change your toilet of choice, or housekeeping, for that matter. Watch out for your best interest. If it is not working for you, change. Use your common sense. Many do not use it. Keep it simple.

There is power in dreaming

To a child there is nothing more powerful than Santa Claus. Back in the fun days when our boys were true believers, we had a friend pop by on the back deck at a strategic time all dressed up in the red suit. After a huge amount of excitement, we were quizzing our son how Santa would ever get back up the chimney once he got down. Almost dancing, he pointed to his own nose and exclaimed, "He just points to the side of his nose, and up the chimney he goes. You just never know!"

What am I saying here? I'm not telling you to believe things that are fake or untrue. I'm just saying get excited and get started. Check your attitude as well. Maybe some of your habits need looking at. Start dancing and point to the side of your nose. This is a good part of why I write: I want you to discover your own financial possibilities. Take it from my son, when he was very young and full of dreams. If you follow simple truths, *up the chimney you will go!* You just never know what might happen.

I say that figuratively, of course. Start discussing your dreams with your advisor. Something good will start.

Elephant glue

Why am I focusing on plain, simple truth?

It is easier to glue down small bits one at a time than glue down a whole elephant.

Unless you win a lottery, you will not retire that line of credit with one big, fat check.

The way to eat an elephant is one bite at a time.

Chapter Six

FINANCIAL ENEMIES

What is this, some kind of war?

People today seem a bit hawkish when it comes to money. They may even be a bit nervous. We have been taught the love of it can lead to all kinds of trouble. Most of us can think of a case of money trouble in either family or among friends. Perhaps trouble has appeared in your own life. We have all heard the saying "Money cannot buy happiness," but somehow innately, we know lack of it certainly can bring hardship. We have witnessed it.

Our cute little neighbours

Our beloved friend the squirrel has a small brain capacity but has the smarts in the summer and fall to start preparing for the winter by burying loot. Isn't that a story your mother told you? Mine certainly did, but it was not quite like her talk with me about the "pistils and the stamens." Yikes! That talk on the birds and the bees was quite the memorable occasion, to say the least. And all I did was ask a simple question about a belly button, *and it opened Pandora's box!* (Well, you get what I mean.) The part of the talk I remember best was some guy playing the bagpipes down the street during the talk. "Okay, Mom, I get it! Enough! Please, this is painful!"

Let's get back to the squirrel story. These little guys bury their loot in times of relative plenty, all in anticipation for a time when it is a little difficult to dine out. Well, it may well not be cognitive, but instinct is definitely inbred. Something many humans lack. What is it that gets in the way of us using our brains? Maybe it is that "cool and drool" thing. The three little pigs comes to mind. One of the little pigs, just like the squirrel, possessed a quality of insight. He had the fortitude to postpone immediate gratification for the purpose of a better future.

On charlatans

Built into our "radar screen" is a protection system. Something my wife calls her crap detectors. It is something acquired over your life experience from charlatans that have lurked in your bushes. They want your loot and don't want to work much to get it; they want something for nothing. Modern-day pirates!

Several years ago, my wife and I had the misfortune of someone throwing a brick through our basement window while we were away. The thieves entered covertly through the broken window in the wee hours of the morning. I have a better word than *turkeys* for them. It won't be printed. After police located us at the beach, we returned to find our home torn apart, a horrific mess, and anything easily pawned was gone. There was no malicious damage to the property; it was profit these pirates were after. They wanted anything that was easily pawned or converted to cash. The police said the breaking and entering was likely to obtain money to fill a drug habit. I would say this would be a plug for home security systems. Don't buy one after the fact, like I did.

We already talked about Bernie Madoff. There are all kinds of pirates like him out there. These charlatans spoil the type of trust that was common in the good old days. They don't care either. But they certainly would take all your loot if they could get away with it.

ROLF ELIASON

Telemarketers

The phone rings. It's getting close to your dinnertime, and the probability of another telemarketer call is around 98.6 percent. These guys usually want your money, but I have even seen ones that want your time. "Just start selling our line, and you are the lucky one that will . . ." Here's a better line, or at least an ironic one: "I'm not selling anything. Just let me give you a free quote . . ." Uh-huh. Enough said. Click.

God bless call display! There is no better way to weed that junk out. Somehow, it seems we are in some kind of war. A war to hang on to the hard-earned equity that we have put together, and everyone wants a part of it.

The little red hen

You may recall me writing about my days bouncing on my mother's knee. One of the favorite stories that she read was "The Little Red Hen." The hen wanted to know who would help her bake her loaf. "Not I!" said the duck. If you don't know the story, please run to the children's section of the bookstore and buy it. It is one of the best financial lessons you will teach your children: *Everyone wants the profits, but no one cares to put the work into making the profits from hard work.*

So what is your opinion?

I once was doing a financial presentation in front of a group of people and gave an introduction to the topic of financial enemies, in a way much similar to the previous number of paragraphs. Here was my starting question: "How many of you here can tell me the greatest financial enemy that you will ever have in your life?"

The first one mentioned was mortgage

Several hands shot up. One eager participant in the front asked if it was a mortgage. I replied, "Good answer. But let's talk about that a little bit." I then went on to share from my own experience how great an enemy interest payments are on the long-term growth of your net worth. Many people have not taken note of how interest payments work or how it affects their wealth. They know they really want the house; they also know somehow the banks would be paid interest. But just how much interest would the banks be getting? They haven't crunched enough numbers to understand what exactly they are signing up for.

The following lesson is one I learned back in the early eighties, when my wife and I purchased our first home. I won't get political here, so I won't name the government party in power at the time. The government introduced a tight money policy, and interest rates went skyrocketing through the roof.

As an aside, at one point early in the eighties, there were savings bonds for sale actually paying 20 percent! What the average person was not aware of is that inflation was actually running at 8 percent at the time. Using the math I described in chapter 1, my break-even point for a tax-adjusted real rate of return on buying these bonds was 11 percent. So if you think I made 20 percent, guess again. My investment was robbed by both inflation and taxation.

Back to the mortgage: the current rates then were around 19 percent. That is no typographical error. They actually were 19 percent! Desperately trying to address falling sales, some builders were offering a much lower rate on a portion of the mortgage for three years as an incentive for prospective buyers to step into the quagmire of high interest rates. What was my lesson? After making the purchase, we paid thirty-six monthly payments, and *only one of those thirty-six payments came off the balance owing when we had to renegotiate.* "What? I made thirty-six payments!" I both questioned and exclaimed. A big moment of truth hit me.

Once again, banks make money. I quickly got out the calculator and started crunching numbers. What I wanted to understand was the degree to which the monthly payment went to cover interest in the early part of the mortgage as opposed to paying down debt. I also discovered the banks would receive *multiple times of the total we borrowed* over the course of the twenty-five years, not just a part or equal portion of what we borrowed. And it would take over eighteen years of the twenty-five year mortgage to pay off half of the balance owing! Isn't half of twenty-five twelve and a half? This again was a big moment of truth. Or to better describe it, a wake-up call!

No, your biggest financial enemy is not your mortgage

Again, I complimented this man's response but then added, "As severe a draw it is on your cash flow, mortgage payments are not your greatest financial enemy. I hear that the cost of an average price of a home in Toronto is nearly five-and-a-half times the average annual Toronto household income. And it is worse on the West Coast. Your mortgage is not insignificant, but it is not your biggest lifetime financial enemy."

Car payments

Someone else asked if it would be car payments. I shook my head and replied, "Well, let's at least talk about it. I am not an expert in that field, but I have bought quite a few cars for myself over the years and have leased as well. I have never sold cars as a profession. It takes a certain breed of individual, and there are many that are very good at it. I thought at one time of going the route of car sales as a career, but the forks in the road took me elsewhere. However, having bought a few cars, I have become familiar with some of the nuances of car ownership."

Depreciation

My father was a highway contractor in a limited partnership with his brother in Alberta, building roads across the province with Caterpillar equipment during the fifties, sixties, and seventies. They knew firsthand the ravages of a financial enemy called depreciation. Purchasing large pieces of heavy equipment is not small business, and they eventually were owners of the equipment through lease-to-own.

Essentially, they rented the graders, dozers, and buggies until they were eventually owned.

Dad approached me one day to ask if I would like to continue in his business. It was his form of succession planning. To me it seemed to be a courtesy gesture, given my young age, but I did appreciate him asking me. Knowing the very competitive nature of the business concerning successful bids for government contracts, I replied, "I know how to run every piece of equipment you have, but I do not have a clue about running your business. I'm off to school." He smiled.

Nearing the end of their successful careers in road building, my father and his brother decided to liquidate their construction equipment and sold by auction through a well-known national equipment auctioneer. Interest rates had gone through the roof, government money was tight, and very few construction jobs were available to bid upon.

The going price my father and his brother achieved in the sale of the equipment (accounting for the number of hours on the equipment) was roughly 10 percent. That is not the commission rate of the auctioneer! That's what the owners pocketed from the sale of the equipment, compared to the original purchase price. Yes, the basic economic law of supply and demand were at work. More importantly, an evil enemy called depreciation was also at work.

Cars are subject to the same enemy. My father preached the avails of depreciation to me, and gave me a deep respect for this silent but deadly enemy. It is my understanding that new cars may depreciate as much as 20 to 25 percent per year. At that rate of depreciation, a car that you buy today would be worth only half of what you paid for it in only two years! What? Look at the book value of the car. Here is the math: $X (1 - 0.25) * (1 - 0.25) = 0.56 * X$, just a smidgeon over half what you bought it for! If you are lucky enough for it to only depreciate 20 percent each year, it would still be worth less than two-thirds of what you bought it for two years previous. It is my opinion cars are a major sinkhole for your cash. And many people achieve "big hat, no cattle" status, courtesy of buying far more cars than they need. Beware.

Meanwhile, back at the seminar, and sticking to sizzle, not the steak, I responded to this gentleman. I remind you, he believed car payments to be his worst financial enemy. I looked directly at the gentleman, but my comments were to all there: "Most, if not all, of you here have the experience of what you paid for an upfront purchase, your monthly payment or lease cost in acquiring the privilege to drive a car. You may even have taken out the calculator to see what your full costs are. Shocking as that might be to you, car payments are not your biggest financial enemy."

The smart remark

From the back of the room a hand shot up. "I know the answer to the question. It's my wife!" *Brave man, she wasn't there to hear his cocky answer.* After the snickering across the room settled, I began to talk about his answer and talk as well a bit about my own life.

"I hear you, buddy, but you may or may not be completely serious." He did bring up a good point, though. Having a spouse that is frugal is a bigger asset than you may realize. Recall what we touched on earlier about peoples' attitude changes with the level of their bank statement. It also changes when there is a change in cash flow, like a raise at work.

We also touched on the fact that it is not a particular transaction that may land that white elephant in your room; it is the continuation of bad habits that leads to its presence. If you are married to a spouse that is a spendthrift that squanders cash lying around, find a way to put the cash away. Out of sight and out of mind.

I believe this can be a very sensitive area for some, especially if one is frugal and the other is a spendthrift or absolutely loves shopping. I mean, isn't it really a balance? Yes, my Wizard of Cause would answer. There are extremes in any issue, and it really boils down to close communication. It is about being on the same page.

I recall being out at a farm kitchen table, discussing with my clients items concerning their finance. Do you think money can't cause dissension between spouses? Guess again! I was a bit embarrassed for the vivid discussion taking place between them over a financial issue. The argument continued at great length, when the retired hobby farmer exclaimed to his wife in frustration, "Woman! I'm going to take you out to the barn!" He wasn't serious, but he was seriously concerned over the issue.

Money can divide itself. It can also divide relationships.

Moving on in the seminar, I thanked him and sensed it was time that I bring the big surprise out of the bag.

Welcome to Canada Revenue Agency

I then made the announcement: "The biggest drain on your finances is taxation. Period!" I don't think anyone in the room was very surprised with my announcement, even though several suggestions had already been made. It is kind of like the plain, simple truth. "Oh yes, I can see that." I went on to explain.

It is my understanding that before World War I, in Canada, there was no such thing as personal income tax. That is hard to believe, isn't it? Can you imagine not having any personal income tax? Even though the thought intrigues me, I still would rather live today, complete with taxation, thank you very much. Initially, the government was caught with paying for an extremely expensive war, and here was a great solution. "Why stop a good thing from going?" asked the government of the day. "Or growing?"

Taxation happens not only at the federal level but provincial as well. If you are a property owner, you will face property taxes as well. Aren't you glad there is not another level of government?

Today we have progressive marginal tax rates. The more you make, the more they progressively take. I surmise the thinking is the more you make, the more you can proportionally afford. Marginal rates even vary from province to province.

So what do we do about our biggest financial enemy?

That is one of the best questions asked in this book. In fact, the question is so important that I have designated one full chapter to the answer. I'll bet you can't wait to get to the next chapter! But our world has many financial enemies, and it would be wise to make note of them. Yes, this is a bit more of the plain, simple truth, but we really are in a war for your financial success. Here are a few more financial enemies.

Lack of implementation

I actually had a person in my office brag, "I have the best plan, and it was put together for me by my accountant." After talking with this client, and after I began discussing with her the issue of living within her means, it was clear to me that "cool and drool" was fast at play in her life. She had no intention of living within her means, nor had she any intention of implementing what the accountant had laid out for her. Ladies and gentlemen, *a plan without appropriate action is of no use*. However, I am grateful to this client for the additional example for this book.

Procrastination

It is bad financial news to ignore a series of actions that need to be taken. It is almost as bad as saying, "Not now!" Have you ever heard the saying that time is money? It stems from that same formula we discussed earlier with time as the exponent. Procrastination is sometimes deliberate. Other times it is from just not paying due attention. Either way, the formula stands. Time is money. If your advisor is prodding you to take action, you need to do something even if it hurts a bit. If you can put up with a dentist's drill, knowing it is your best interest, then you can listen to your financial advisor. If he or she is worth a pinch of salt, he or she has your best interest at heart.

Lack of planning

Worse yet is someone who has no clue about how to get started and no plan to follow. I recently was in a city with which I was slightly familiar but became somewhat turned around and had a schedule to meet. I had already stopped for directions. You likely have been there in a similar situation. Have you ever noticed some people are challenged when it comes to giving directions? Fortunately, I eventually came across people that knew the area well and were concise with directions. You need the same type of people for financial direction. Find a financial advisor you can work well with who will put in place a plan specific to your needs. Ask for a plan. Follow it.

The cycle of market emotions

Within our industry several of the wholesalers have distributed a piece of literature I find very intriguing, and it is a plain, simple truth. It is called the cycle of market emotions. This page shows a sinusoidal curve depicting investor sentiment as market conditions change. That investor might be you! Initially, the investor is optimistic of the condition of the market; otherwise, he or she would not invest. As the market improves, so does his excitement. Much like "I'm on a roll!" in Las Vegas. Right at the top of the market movement is the point of maximum risk, and the investor is elated.

"Sell now? Are you kidding?" As the market movements recede, the investor starts justifying to himself, "I'm a long-term investor!" It worsens, and as it does, the investor's emotion turns to one of "Maybe I should never have invested!" The market falls further and the investor becomes despondent, almost to the point of capitulation. He or she then asks, "How much would it cost if I sold out right now?" This is actually the point of maximum opportunity, and the investor's emotion is opposite to the situation. The market eventually returns, and the investor's sentiment returns to what he started with. The point of the story is that your emotion has nothing to do with smart investing. Again, talk to your advisor.

ROLF ELIASON

The clock is ticking

I asked my mother when I was young why my hair was blond and both her hair and my father's were dark. I seriously was worried about how this could be. Her response to me was "Oh, don't you worry about that. It will grow darker when you grow up." Well, Mom, I guess I didn't grow up. It is still blond. Only thing is, it is starting to go gray. Hey, wait a minute! I didn't think blonds could go gray! I am discovering otherwise. It is also falling out. But you will never ever find me wearing a wig!

The fact is, when you are born, you are born to eventually die. I am not talking morbidly here; I am facing fact. We as advisors face it especially when talking estate planning or life insurance. You really do need to prepare for your future, including the event of your death. We will be looking at that more carefully in chapters that follow, but suffice it to say that some things need tending to, perhaps sooner than later. You have no guarantees of making it to tomorrow, let alone to the age your parents lived.

We have all heard stories of tragedy, and most go on the assumption that it will never happen to us. It just might. Your assets have taken a lifetime to accumulate. You have all kinds of enemies. Perhaps you should do something to protect those assets and the people you love.

Chapter Seven

SLAY THE DRAGON

I am a little uneasy writing this chapter. I do not consider myself an extraordinary man. However, this extraordinary dragon can morph. Tax laws are complicated and in a continual state of flux. I hope to stick to plain, simple truth and sell sizzle. "Go while the going is good." Some things change with time. The dragon is one of them.

Branding

If you have ever been in my office, you might have noticed that I have made an attempt at branding my practice. I have done the best job that I can to present a theme, conveying in a subtle way what I am really about. As you look about the room, you will see some of the individual items I have chosen and included about the room. You will begin to recognize a theme.

I have a couple of chairs for visiting guests in front of my desk, with a round coffee table between the chairs. This makes it convenient for clients to place personal items such as documents they may have brought along with them or personal items like a purse. It is not really the furniture I wish to focus upon, although I have tried to make any visit as pleasant an experience as possible. It is the icons about the room that I wish to tell you about.

ROLF ELIASON

The Viking ship

I was born Canadian but of Scandinavian heritage. My father was of Swedish heritage, and my mother was of Norwegian, although she was born and raised in Wisconsin. I have always been taught to be proud of my heritage, and for the most part I am. I am most proud being Canadian. Let's not focus on the fact of my Viking ancestors looting and pillaging. It happened hundreds of years ago, according to history books, but it did happen.

Have you ever heard of the Swedish toast to your good health? You may have heard it used before: "Skol!" Apparently, my ancestors were a bloodthirsty lot, cutting off the heads of their enemies. In celebration, they would scrape out the gray matter, fill the skull with their alcoholic brew, and toast their success, "Skol!" And if you believe that one, I have many other stories to tell.

You should Google *Leif Erickson* to get a clear picture. It was during a visit to St. Anthony, Newfoundland, that a controversial item of history was confirmed for me. I had been taught otherwise in school, just as had many others. Leif Ericson was on the Rock (more commonly known as Newfoundland) in AD 900. This was long before Christopher Columbus made his debut in 1492. Christopher Columbus discovered America? Apparently not!

The curator of Parks Canada for this site was in the main building where we visited. I disclosed to him my Viking heritage and asked him if he would like to hear a very short Swedish poem I had been taught regarding Columbus. He asked me if the poem was short. I assured him it was very short indeed and then recited the following to him in a fake Swedish accent: "In 1492, Columbus discovered—Hullabaloo!" The curator loved it!

Okay, back to my office. A fairly prominent Viking ship created artistically from various pieces of metal is mounted on the wall. My wife and I purchased it at a Danish teak furniture store shortly after we were married. On the back of this three-dimensional piece of art I have placed a cute little Viking man at the rudder I call Sven. Sven was purchased at one of the many Newfoundland shops we visited. He comes complete with a Viking hat, sword, armor, hair braids, and full mustache.

There is also a model of a lighthouse that sits on the coffee table. On the wall above my desk is a clock in the form of a brass ship's wheel. It gives you that "at the helm" kind of feeling.

A cherished painting

An original painting that once belonged to the Wizard of Cause graces one of the walls, an original modern-day oil painting depicting a sailing vessel, less the sails and beached on the sand. Every time I look at the painting, I think of him.

Several other icons

The vestibule features a few small icons. There's a small cubical piece of rock from Newfoundland, painted to model one of the many wildly colourful saltbox homes in St. John's. A small model of a Newfoundland dory is on the same shelf as the rock. There is also a relatively large wooden fish carved in a modern style as well as a carved wooden charging bull. I love to fish, and the charging bull keeps me charged with dreams of positive market movement.

If the ship theme wasn't prominent enough, I also have a model ship of the *Bluenose*, a sailing vessel very famous within Canadian history, on top of the vestibule. To understand how famous it is, look at the dime in your pocket. This vessel, the *Bluenose*, is engraved on it. I purchased the model in the gift shop of the *Chi-Cheemaun* ferry running in Ontario between the Bruce Peninsula and Manitoulin Island. Why would I go to such lengths of depicting such a theme? Well, I think you may have already observed—I am a storyteller. It probably comes from bouncing on my mother's knee.

The captain

I have one last icon I want to tell you about, which will tie this all together. It was also purchased in a gift shop in Newfoundland. Do you mind if I give a plug for visiting Newfoundland? I just did! Go there, for it is an unforgettable experience. You will not be disappointed! The sights are amazing. The people there are truly awesome. If only you could understand their accent! "Yes, b'y!"

This last but not least important icon with which I will test your patience is a little figurine strategically and centrally placed in the vestibule. It is in a location that is prominently lit by a halogen light and likely first catching your eye.

The figurine is that of a man in a captain's hat holding nautical charts and looking through a sextant. You may have already guessed it. I'm the guy. Captain Rolf! The underlying message: "This guy is looking out for your best interest. It is easy to get lost, and there are dangers around!"

So it all kind of ties in together: A sea of investment and of danger. / Rowing about the sea with your dory boat of savings. / Dangers lurk! / The lighthouse is there for your protection. / Captain Rolf has his charts and instruments.

I think you get the idea. Okay, I beat it to death. Oh yes, and there is the name of this book. What is it with my obsession with water? Rivers, lakes, seas . . . Do you think I will someday retire by some form of water? Good question. Remember Jane and Henry Fonda in *On Golden Pond*? They had no clue the rock was just below the surface, and whammo! Okay, I get it! Like my son said, "Dad! Move on!"

The whole branding thing is purposed to convey the message that investing, though full of adventure, can also be dangerous. We have already identified Canada Revenue Agency as the largest financial drain you will have during your entire life. What is a sailor to do? The dragon we are going to slay is *taxation you may not need to be paying*. Really? Why would anyone pay taxes they need not pay? It is happening more than you think! You may have a dragon in your boat and not even realize it. They morph, remember?

All taxation is not the same

Taxation is set at different rates for different levels of income. This is reflected in various marginal tax rates, which vary from province to province. Those marginal rates also vary according to your total income. There is another way in which taxation is applied differently. The way in which your funds grow has a great influence on how the growth is taxed.

Interest income

Growth that comes from interest is taxed in the same way as remuneration, or wages. Interest income is one of the worst ways you can receive growth, tax-wise. It is fully taxed at your marginal tax rate, as we discussed earlier. The more you make in a given year in income, the higher your marginal tax rate is.

But wait—there is more!

The Wizard of Cause taught me at an early age that there are two other means of investment growth called capital gains and dividends. Capital gains and dividends are a preferable means of growth, being taxed at a lower level. A tax preferred in your eyes, not in the eyes of Revenue Canada. They want your money, and if they can get away with it politically and not lose their job, they will do it. Think of pirates. Or the guy that threw the brick through my basement window. They want your loot. Lower taxes are better, right? That would mean more money in your pocket? Sizzle . . .

So here it is. The three weapons you have to reduce your taxes are

- Defer
- Convert
- Avoid

Does this seem simple to you? What, may I ask, is so bad about plain, simple truth? Let's discuss these three friends and how you might employ them.

Defer your tax bill—don't pay now, pay it later

When you are paying a tax bill, it is much better to pay the taxes later. Don't pay them now if you don't have to! The question is, who is getting the utility of using the capital during that time, you or the government? Better put, whose money is it anyway? Who worked for it? Wouldn't you rather have money grow in your pocket than in theirs? If it is legal, by all means pay later! However, you must stay within the law. Perhaps something seems morally right to you, but if it is not legal, it will not fly. Have you ever played Monopoly? You might get a *do not pass go and go directly to jail*.

Registered plans

There are several ways of delaying the payment of your tax bill while remaining legal. One is through a Registered Retirement Savings Plan. The government was the one that invented it! RSPs work best for the sole purpose they were designed: improving your retirement income. Unfortunately, far too few Canadians take advantage of this tax-deferral mechanism. This type of plan allows all growth—interest, dividends, and capital gains—to accumulate on a tax-deferred basis, usually until you retire. You pay the tax only as you deregister your funds from the plan.

Many critics of RSPs usually point to the fact that when funds are deregistered, they are taxed fully as income at your marginal tax rate. What these critics either don't know or ignore is that when you retire, *your marginal tax rate is usually at a lower rate* than when you were contributing to the plan. Many people focus only on one thing when they make their contribution: the RSP contribution receipt, or the deduction from their taxable income that year. Don't get me wrong, this is definitely a tax advantage through deferral. However, I believe the relatively lower marginal tax during retirement is more important than the deduction. That would be more money in your pocket at a time when you have your feet up in retirement. Sizzle.

Retirement income funds

By the end of the year in which you turn seventy-one years of age, you must cash your plan in and pay tax on the lot, roll your RSP into an annuity, or roll it over into a RIF, a Retirement Income Fund. Take your pick, one of those three options. A RIF continues your ability to defer taxation. It also allows the monthly deregistration of the assets without facing partial deregistration fees for each redemption.

What is my humble opinion? Option 1 to me seems to be a poor choice. Why would you pay one huge tax bill now at the highest marginal tax rate possible and not later? Option 2 may seem a bit more prudent, but with interest rates at an all-time low, it's a bit of a tough sell. Once the annuity route is chosen, rates remain locked at that level for the remainder of your life. If interest rates begin to climb along with inflation and the cost of living—tough luck! You are contractually obligated to remain at the same rate at the time the annuity was purchased. Your obligation remains until you die.

My choice would be option 3, the RIF, allowing you to keep the same funds you had owned before in a new vehicle. The RIF automatically deposits cash into your bank account while leaving the remainder within the plan. What is smart about that option? It's called tax deferral.

Buy and hold

One means of deferring taxes outside of an RSP is to buy an equity mutual fund that generates capital gains, and do not sell it. Capital gains will not be triggered until you sell the stock.

Another way that taxes may be deferred is by means of business property interests held within a corporation. The owner of the corporation is not required to take all profits from the corporation in a given year. Some of these profits may be left in the company as retained earnings. Many people do not have the luxury of having a business of their own. If you do own one and have not yet incorporated your business, you may want to examine closely the cost versus benefits of incorporating. Tax deferral within a corporation is one of the main advantages of incorporating.

The method you use to defer taxes gives you the advantage of increasing your wealth through that deference and at a much greater rate than you would otherwise achieve. This is more money in your pocket, less worry, and yes, it is legal. Did you notice I just took you from a feature, developed an advantage, and then pointed out your benefit? Once a salesman, always a salesman.

Sizzle . . .

Convert to a tax-favored instrument

The type of investment you choose dictates how it is taxed. Some investors give taxation a brief glance when choosing an investment, shrugging off taxation like it was not important or that it was inevitable. "The government needs our capital for programs, right?" Oh, really? Would you like to get your checkbook out and sign a blank one for Revenue Canada? Investors should be taking a hard look at their full picture. Isn't it what your money will buy that counts? Again, look at your returns after taxation and inflation.

Capital gains

Remember I said this dragon can morph? Capital gains were not always taxed in Canada. They became taxed under major tax reform in January 1972, about the time I was graduating from high school. Originally, any capital gain achieved by a Canadian was taxed at a 50 percent inclusion rate, which meant that only one-half of what you gained would be taxed at your marginal rate. The other half would remain tax-free. I like tax-free, don't you? Do you not wish the other half was not taxed either? Wishful thinking! We should be thankful the first half of it remains tax-free. That is what happens when you convert your income to capital gains. I would rather pay tax on half of my gains than all of it, wouldn't you? I mean, that is the plain, simple truth, is it not?

Tax laws are always in a state of change. In 1990, capital gains inclusion into taxable income went to a 75 percent level, staying that way for about ten years. In 2000, it was lowered to 66.67 percent, but in October of the same year, it fell back to the original 50 percent inclusion rate, at which it now still stands.

If you have savings outside of an RSP and you convert your savings from interest income into capital gains, you certainly will realize tax savings. You really do not want to pay tax at full inclusion on these nonregistered assets, do you? Beware of one caveat: *When you go to capital gains from interest income, your investment risk usually has increased*. It is not just about taxation, but it is also about what risk are you taking. Once again, do not roll the dice; talk to your investment advisor. You must look at the whole picture and determine an allocation appropriate for your objectives, risk tolerance, and risk capacity.

Dividends

I am not a tax expert. I leave that to my accountant. I will attempt to explain this type of growth in a simple manner. Another means of converting to tax-favored instruments is by choosing mutual funds that pay dividends each month, quarterly, semiannually, or even annually. If your fund is outside of an RSP, you will receive a T-3 (generated by a trust structure) or a T-5 (generated by a corporation structure). These forms would arrive in the spring from the mutual fund company, outlining those dividends paid out during the year.

Be careful of when you buy dividend-paying funds

A big surprise may come to those that purchase dividend-paying mutual funds late in the year in a nonregistered account. Dividends are often paid out in December, and for those that purchase dividend-paying mutual funds, be very careful of purchasing late in the year. Why? The value of the fund may drop with market fluctuations, and with a possible pay out of dividends, you may look at your year-end statement, find the value less than what you invested, yet end up with a nasty T-3 or a T-5 for dividends paid.

Paying taxes, when the value of your funds is less than what you first invested, is a nasty surprise. However, it is a different story for mutual funds purchased within an RSP; all dividends are not taxed until withdrawal from the plan, usually many years later, and often in a lower marginal tax rate. What is the moral of the story? Purchase your dividend-paying mutual funds in nonregistered assets early in the year, not at the end of the year. Wait until the dividend has been paid, and then buy. This is not market timing. We are avoiding taxable distributions and keeping it simple by buying these funds early in the year, not later.

Dividends paid during the taxation year on nonregistered funds must be declared that taxation year. My argument is that you will come out much further ahead in your taxes than you would have if the gain was in interest income alone. Yes, there is a gross up of the dividend, but the rate at which they are taxed improves. There is the distinct advantage of a dividend tax credit, lowering your tax bill. Sizzle again!

Avoid

Let me be clear. Pay all taxes that you are legally required to pay. Certainly, I am not talking about tax evasion. That could eventually land you in jail. I am speaking of using every legal means available to not pay taxes on some things earned. The onus is upon you to avoid every tax you need not pay. How would you do that?

TFSAs

We have already spoken about the use of TFSAs, or tax-free savings accounts. Did you notice the word *free*? That would be a good word when describing your taxes. I believe this saving vehicle is most important for young people. I often get the question of whether their savings should go into their TFSA or their RSP. Which vehicle will place them further ahead?

It depends. If the individual is not making a huge amount of income at that point in their life and they are young, I would say the TFSA route would be better for them. Tax-free wins over tax-deferred. It also depends on the intention of use. If the funds are for retirement savings, the RSPs make them more difficult to get at and less likely to be redeemed. That is to say, when you deregister RSP assets, they become taxable, and depending on the size of the redemption, withholding tax will have to be paid. Withholding tax is essentially a prepayment against taxes due in the spring. With TFSAs, what you see on your statement is what you may utilize, less any deferred sales charges.

TFSAs have already been mentioned and are not to be looked upon in the same manner as a bank account. There are specific rules as to how much you may contribute per year, along with redemption and payback rules, which may or may not include penalties. Another word for *tax*, would you not agree?

For people in a higher marginal tax rate, an RSP wins over the TFSA as long as the purpose of the investment is long-term growth or retirement savings. If you want tax-free growth that you may utilize in the next few years, go the TFSA route. The bottom line is, if you can afford, contribute both to RSP and TFSA. Utilizing both is ideal.

Business expenses

You can usually identify which people are in business for themselves by how carefully they retain receipts. Receipts for business lunches, receipts for items purchased at the office supply store, and certainly receipts at the gas station for their fuel. These receipts provide deductions resulting in taxes not owed. If a person ditches the gas receipt before getting back in the car, I know they are likely not in business for themselves.

One of the main perks in being in your own business is the deduction of valid business expenses from earned income. Any activity that occurs in moving the company forward is a legitimate deduction, hence the dedicated retention of receipts. The government often requests proof of these deductions. When money is involved, some like to push the envelope.

Windup of dragon-slaying

I wrote at the very beginning of this book that I would attempt to stick to simplicity. Composing this chapter has been challenging for me as the nature of the topic lends itself to more specifics and detail. I hope you gleaned the most important, wonderful tax friends we have:

- Defer

- Convert

- Avoid

Slay the dragon! He is your worst financial enemy, and if you don't do something about him, he will gladly take your loot. Why? You may have forgotten to use legal means already in place to keep him at bay. Or perhaps you didn't think about it much.

Now you have no excuse.

Chapter Eight

+PIT, −FIT

Why do people abbreviate or use acronyms? An acronym tends to be easier to remember than all the words at once. Sometimes the titles can be cleverly chosen so that the acronym actually makes sense and is easier to remember. The title of an organization or program implemented often has several names that are difficult to remember, all contributing to what it stands for or a goal that is placed. Once the acronym is in place, it becomes much easier to remember the rest. That is the reason for the title of this chapter.

I have a little secret I want to let you in on. I have a secret formula for making money. I am very serious! To my knowledge, no one else to date has come up with this formula. I was going to construct an acronym without periods and the dash, but when I Googled *PITFIT*, I found that someone else has already used it to name their fitness program for motocross training. I do not want to step on anyone's toes!

I tried reversing it to *FITPIT* but again found someone with a technique to become fit through boxing. Again, I did not want to upset anyone using a term already spoken for. I modified it—just a little. I am not trying to trademark anything. I just want to draw your attention to something you really, really need to know.

So, ladies and gentlemen, here it is: +PIT, −FIT. This secret formula has nothing to do with a name of a company or trade secret from which I am going to profit. That is why I am giving it out. What a nice guy I am. No charge! I am sure I have you wondering what the letters mean.

The six letters represent six items you must account for to make a real rate of return, or quantify your *actual* benefit, not just the one you initially perceive. Let's discuss this for a moment. There is a basic difference between truth and opinion. I want to be very, very clear: *truth is independent of opinion, although the opinion may well be in line with truth.*

The same is true for your actual benefit versus your perceived benefit. You may not understand your actual benefit simply because you did not know the full picture or were misinformed. Paul Harvey, a former, well-known journalist, would often say, "And now you know . . . *the rest of the story!*" So what is the rest of the story?

No exceptions, all six variables count in the formula. What I am getting at is the real return on your investment after fees, inflation, and taxes are accounted for. *What will your profit actually do for you?*

Remember the Hannigan's burger for thirty-five cents? Would I have been able to buy the burger if the government had first taken a dime in tax and Mr. Hannigan had charged an extra nickel service charge? Probably not! What mattered to me was the burger, not the dime and the quarter. Just remember, if I had an extra dime and a nickel taken from me back then, it meant a lot more than it does today. I might not have enjoyed the hamburger, and kept fifty cents. That would be the thirty-five cents plus fifteen cents of surcharge.

On the positive side

We have already visited the formula for future value (capital invested plus all financial gain), including principal (what is invested) and a couple more variables, interest (rate of return) and time (compounding periods).

Time represents the compounding period, depending if the interest rate quoted is compounded annually, or semiannually. It indicates the number of times the increase is multiplied upon itself along with the original principal invested. Herein is the beauty of compounding. Most people have a fair understanding of these three variables: principal, interest, and time. They also know they have to give their investment time to grow but seem to focus inordinately upon the rate of return. The principal contributed and time required to attain what they wish, for the most part, seem to be ignored. Don't forget our story about the Little Red Hen. Rate of return is what comes their way. Principal contributed and waiting for results is tough work.

P *is for principal*

Investors know they have to place some capital at risk to make an investment. That would be their initial investment, or capital, they have placed at risk. It takes money to make money. This statement is full of plain, simple truth. The larger the principal you start with, the more the rate has an effect in absolute dollars. Therefore, 5 percent of a million dollars is $50,000, but 5 percent of a thousand dollars is only $50. The capital you end up with is directly proportional to what you start with. Starting with more means you end with more. This is plain, simple truth.

I *is for interest*

Interest is usually specified and at a rate compounded either semiannually or annually. If the number of times it is compounded per year is not specified, and you are depositing money, you can rest assured it will only be compounded annually. If you owe money, you should look very closely if the compounding is done more than once per year. Gee, those bankers are smart! Does this not remind you of Revenue Canada charging you interest when you owe them money but not paying you any interest if they owe you? It doesn't seem right.

To determine your eventual capital result, including growth, the following factor is multiplied to the initial investment: one plus the interest rate is raised to the number of times of compounding. If it is compounded annually, that exponent would be the number of years you leave it in place.

T is for time

Money is time; time is money. You have heard that quoted many times. It is very true. Of the three variables that make you money, *this is the all-important one*. That is why advisors talk about starting early. That is why advisors often preach to stay the course. That is why Albert Einstein called compound interest one of the wonders of the world. It is so powerful; it is almost like magic, but it isn't. It is a cold, hard mathematical fact. I cannot emphasize how important it is that young people be made aware of how powerful this is. Young people have one of the most powerful tools available: their time horizon. My Wizard of Cause knew this well. That is why he approached me to start saving at age twenty-five. Just because! Here we go again . . .

What happens if we have less of one of these three variables? There had better be more of the other two, or the result will not be there. It takes all three. I remind you that the time element is the exponent and refers to the number of times it is compounded. Thus, the time element is the most significant of the three.

On the negative side

What? There is a negative side to making money? Regretfully, there is! Many investors do not take time to look outside the box and look at the full picture. What really counts in an investment? "Return!" you would likely answer. But what is it that you mean? Have you accounted for everything?

I keep bringing up the Hannigan's burger, but I believe it is a good example. At the point of purchase, it was the burger that was important to me, not the thirty-five cents. Especially when I was hungry on a Friday night! What really matters in investment is what your investment will do for you. Once again, focus on your benefit. Sizzle!

That would be called purchasing power. You really do have to look at everything that is taken away from you. Look at how inflation has affected your overall picture. Preferably you have been watching it as time has moved on. Some of you will have better stories than I on the effects of inflation. I just remembered the ten-cent soft ice cream cone I used to enjoy. Yes, three negative variables must also be accounted for when you are talking about making money: fees, inflation, and taxation.

F *is for fees*

A whole book could be written for arguments that are taking place in our business over this issue at the time. I do wish to discuss this in more depth because it certainly does affect you. It is the cost of your participation with the mutual fund company and your advisor. That is how they are paid. I easily get tired from mudslinging at financial advisors by financial critics in the newspapers.

These critics tend to focus on two areas of charge that clients face. I challenge these people who preach on top of the apple box provided by the newspaper. The issue at hand is whether or not the financial advisor has given the client a full disclosure of fees that are paid to the fund company.

It does not satisfy or appease those critics that the fees are fully disclosed in the prospectus. A prospectus must be delivered with each sale. They also ignore the fact that advisors are discussing with their clients how they themselves are paid or how a deferred sales charge works. They want the exact dollars and cents charged by the dealer printed on every client statement.

Now wait a minute! I have a question.

How would this be any different than demanding the newspaper print on every newspaper be the salary of the critic? I paid for his salary with my subscription! I want to see if I am getting value for the money I am paying. It is doubtful that would happen, but is it not the same issue? Like the French would say in a match of sword fighting: *"Touché!"*

These fees are taken right off the top by the mutual fund company to cover costs before any results are published in the media. It is not possible to purchase funds with absolutely no fees of any kind. Think of it—would a fund manufacture a fund and give service without being paid? Never!

ROLF ELIASON

Would you like to work for nothing? Never! Come on, that is the direct opposite of a pirate. Let me do some work for you for nothing! You might do that for a friend or family member out of love, but that is not the way business works. Business only continues where profit is made. If your dealer has presented your funds as "no fee" and has not discussed management expense ratios, he has not given you the full picture. A fundamental law of business is you do not get something for nothing.

Fees, continued—management expense ratios

This hidden charge by the fund company is called the management expense ratio, or MERs. MERs are fees charged by the fund companies to pay for many costs they face, such as accounting, legal, and trustee fees. The fund manager also must be paid, along with distribution costs as well. Some of these distribution costs include a portion of the MER. It is paid to the dealer in the form of a trail, which compensates the dealer for their business and keeps the advisor willing to continue service.

The argument of MERs, or management expense ratios, being too high is a different issue, but high compared to what? Consider something called economy of scale. Often these critics compare Canada's MERs to those mutual funds our neighbors to the south purchased in the USA. Many of their funds are ten times the size of ours in capitalization, and their population is also ten times what ours is. It is not a fair comparison. We have a free market system with many fund companies competing with each other for their share of the business. They compete not just on returns but also on the cost of their service. This cost of service is passed on to the client through the MER charged.

There is no collusion. Mutual fund companies are in competition with each other. In my opinion, the MERs are where they are because that is where they need to be. If a fund company comes in with a very attractively low MER for the client, don't think for a moment the advisor has not taken notice. We have our tools and charts, and looking at what the client is being charged for the service is a fiduciary responsibility. This is a definite consideration in modeling a cost effective portfolio for the client. Better returns, less cost, and more sizzle for the client.

The argument that the chartered financial analysts (who run these mutual funds) are not adding enough return for managing the pool of capital is another complaint they raise. I once suffered a sudden loss in that stock I had poorly chosen for my own holdings. The experience for me was, to say the least, enlightening. What was the lesson for me? Experience counts for more than we realize. It gets back to what the Wizard of Cause was telling me: "Look for an expert and use his expertise, even if a reasonable cost is incurred."

I found that purchase to be a far faster ride than that of a pool of capital being run in a mutual fund by a CFA, a chartered financial analyst. These are the experts hired by the mutual fund company to manage the pool of capital in a manner congruent with the mutual fund prospectus. I am a mutual fund salesperson, and I gladly pay the MERs in funds I personally own to pay for expertise in downside protection. In fact, downside protection is a particular focus of mine. Do not forget the math I showed you on returning to where you started.

Isn't this one of those "Keep your eye upon the doughnut and not upon the hole" kind of thing? MERs are important, but in my opinion, there are other factors that matter more. For example, long-run return. Often these statistics vary between funds far more than the entire MER! So which factor remains more important? My focus is more on return than cost, although both are important.

Fees continued—deferred sales charges

Another bitter item these newspaper and television critics bring up is deferred sales charges. I will not go into great detail here other than to say these charges lock you into a particular fund company for the length of the schedule and not a particular fund. Switches within the fund company may be made at any time during the deferred sales charge schedule with no charge, such as changing from dividends to a bond type of mutual fund.

These critics continue with their argument, saying no one understands deferred sales charges and no advisor truly discloses what is going on. Well, Mr. Critic, there are Bernie Madoffs out there, but I am not one of them. There is full disclosure with my clients. The cost of participation in these funds is also spelled out in the prospectus, which the investor receives. Is it the mutual fund salesman's fault that the prospectus has been written in such a complicated way? It is challenging to read, and few clients actually read them.

I have a small moral problem with those advisors charging deferred sales charges (DSC) on nonregistered funds. Why? A client may initially claim the purpose of the nonregistered deposit is for long-term capital appreciation. However, the client's needs or wants may change and often do. A mutual fund redemption or partial redemption from funds sold (with a deferred sales charge) will result in a redemption fee charged to the client, as disclosed in the prospectus. This would be for any time period within the redemption schedule, which is usually seven years. I am very reluctant to sell a fund on a DSC schedule if the funds are outside a registered plan for this very reason. However, in RSP funds, it is a different story. These funds are meant for retirement, and often these funds are not touched for the length of the deferred sales schedule.

Should the client change advisor, funds sold on a deferred sales charge could be brought over *in kind* or remain in the same mutual fund. This would result in no deferred sales charges applying. Unless the advisor is forbidden to use the individual funds the prospective client has, the advisor should be bringing the fund over in kind so as not to trigger a new deferred schedule. I think I have spoken loud and clear on fees.

I is for inflation, T is for taxation

The last two negatives, inflation and taxation, we have already spoken of. We spoke at lengths about the thirty-five-cent burger back in the late sixties and how the cost of living has indeed risen at great length.

The government has done a marvelous job at keeping inflation within a 2 to 3 percent target rate within the last twenty years or so. Many of us remember in the early eighties when very large negative effects of inflation existed at a time when assets were often held within interest-bearing vehicles. We also spoke of a means of calculating a break-even point, the point at which you actually increase your after-tax, after-inflation rate of return. This would be better stated as increasing your purchasing power. When you focus on your true after-tax, after-inflation purchasing power, you are focusing on your *real* benefit and not your *perceived* benefit. Ignore these two enemies of inflation and taxation at your peril.

We devoted all of chapter 7 on ways to slay the dragon of taxes. You may not need to be paying some of these taxes. Why would anyone want to? If you are thinking of the social services the government supplies, and that is where you want your money to be earmarked, perhaps you might instead write your charitable check to an organization that you trust. Whom do you trust?

Canadians detest stories of their tax dollars being squandered, and rightly so. I could get into the recent media discussion of our senate and the debate over their expenses and actual place of residence, but then again, I neither want to stray further into a political discussion nor get sued for libel. Truth versus opinion, would you not agree?

In summary, I have given you *my secret formula for making money*: +PIT, −FIT.

+ Principal

+ Interest

+ Time

− Fees

− Inflation

− Taxation

PS: Every one of these six of these variables count!

If your advisor only speaks of the first three, go find yourself one that gives you *the rest of the story*.

Chapter Nine

ANYTHING CAN HAPPEN ANYTIME

I wish to be sensitive in this chapter. I would like to introduce you to one last hero of mine. The last one, I promise. No more photo albums complete with stories. Because of privacy, my hero will remain anonymous. I will not disclose his real name, and his first name will be changed to Dave.

Meeting another hero: first, an advisor

Dave was a financial advisor. He, like I, worked to help people like you. Our number 1 job is to help you achieve your financial goals.

I met Dave at a business meeting in a nearby city one day about six or seven years ago. I had heard by the grapevine that his branch was dissolving. I immediately went into sales mode, talking to him with a focus on his benefit of coming to our branch, alongside several others in the same capacity. After serious consideration, Dave eventually transferred to our branch, and over the course of six or seven years, we became good friends and business colleagues.

We had many discussions surrounding business over lunch, as well as discussing personal goals in detail. Dave liked to work hard and play hard. We discussed items like strategies on how to take risk off the table for a client and improve results. Many clients, having gone through 2008, were eager to reduce their exposure to risk. These items discussed might seem ubiquitous to some, but this is what we do for a living.

A visionary

One of the first things Dave set out to accomplish when he came to our branch was to establish a buy/sell agreement for each advisor in the office. Buy and sell what? Given the event of the death of an advisor, it is the opportunity of appointing beforehand whomever he or she chooses to provide service to his or her clients, with full respect given to the client's wish.

This gives the writer of the agreement the ability to appoint which advisor (whether it be he or she) he felt would be most trusted to step into his or her place to serve his or her clients should the writer of the agreement die.

Why would that be important? Is this overkill? I do not think so; it is all about the "what if?" scenario. Much like life insurance, these agreements would only be acted upon by the death of whoever wrote the agreement. What if one of us should die? What would happen to the clients we look after? What would the surviving spouse be faced with? These were serious questions needing serious answers. When an idea came to Dave's head, he did not waste time to implement the idea but saw it through to completion. Hey, we weren't planning to die. Not at all! We were preparing for the event should it happen. I might add: so should you!

Misread by some

Dave did not win a popularity contest in our branch. Some misread his intentions. He was short on patience and wanted to "Git 'er dun," like we referred to before. He was a no-nonsense type of guy. Even though these intentions might have been misread, I believe his intentions were rock solid. On both fronts, business and social, Dave was a wealth of great ideas. He knew how important it was to have a social event for our branch. In consultation with me, together we decided to organize a yearly barbecue where corn on the cob, hamburgers, and farmer's sausage on a bun would be served, coupled with potluck salad and dessert. There would be plenty of refreshments, plenty of stories, plenty of jokes, and perhaps some bonding all around the pool.

The Rolf Eliason Annual Barbecue and Pool Party

Dave was quick to choose a name for the party social but also noted with a stern face, "We have a problem. There doesn't seem to be a pool at the Eliason home! So let's have the party at my place because I have the pool. But we will keep the title 'The Rolf Eliason Annual Barbecue and Pool Party.'"

Dave took great joy in announcing the party by name to anyone he could and then move closer into their personal space, lowering his voice and asking, "Whose place is it at? Hmmm!" This was classic Dave humor.

The barbecue pool party

He was also the kind of friend that pushed me into the pool at one of these barbecues even though I was fully clothed, wallet and all. It was not just I that became a victim around his pool. On more than a few other occasions, unsuspecting guests would fall victim. He would then explain, usually after pushing his guest into the pool, that the line had definitely been crossed. This line was never seen by anyone else, but it was definitely there. He knew where it was.

I now have experience in drying out bills with a hair dryer. The Queen, with her face on several of the bills, would not be amused. Neither was my wife. However, as surprised as I was, our friendship was not in jeopardy. In a warped way, I started to see the humor, but it wasn't immediate. This was classic Dave. Is this a guy thing? It has to be as my wife viewed it as the same kind of trick as a pie in the face. Slapstick humor! I know she still does not see any humor in it.

THE LAKE OF TWO RIVERS

The start of an unforgettable day

I am telling you these background stories to give you a lead up to one other most notable day in my life, and certainly that of Dave's as well. It was 10:30 a.m. on a sunny Friday in mid-June. "TGIF!" as many would say. Dave called me down to his office as he commonly did to discuss items of business. We entered into a lively discussion surrounding the value of life insurance, and at one point in the discussion, Dave started tapping his finger on his desk.

Anything can happen anytime

Dave had a way with words and would never back away from his opinion. The words he said that morning became etched in my mind, never to be forgotten: "Anything can happen anytime!" He wanted the point to stick, so he leaned over his desk, continued tapping, and repeated, "Anything can happen anytime!" Okay, Dave, point taken.

The Friday afternoon barbecue

It was 11:50 a.m. that same day when Dave said, "Let's talk about this stuff around the pool in my backyard. Who has the pool?" he egged on. Dave absolutely loved to horse around with that line. "You go find a couple of pieces of meat for the barbecue and a bit of salad, and I will go buy some refreshments." Dave and I had on many occasions taken opportunity to discuss business strategy. I believe we both fed off each other's ideas. Little did I realize this would be the last occasion I would talk with him.

We headed off in our cars for the items, with the plan of meeting at his house for the barbecue lunch immediately after purchasing the items. At 12:30 p.m., not much more than half an hour after we had spoken, I was starting to become impatient. *Where is he?* I wondered what the problem was. I phoned Dave's cell, and to my surprise, I was speaking to a police officer. He announced that Dave was in a medical emergency.

What?

I objected, "What kind of emergency? I was just talking with Dave a half an hour ago! We are supposed to have a barbecue together in ten minutes!" I indicated to the officer I was not far from where they were and would be there in less than three minutes. When I arrived, I found the store where Dave had been making his purchase was temporarily closed to the public. Again, I questioned the officer as to exactly what happened to Dave.

The police officer was somewhat noncommittal and would not directly answer my question. He explained he was not medically qualified to answer. He only indicated that it looked like Dave collapsed while waiting in line at the checkout counter of the store where he was making a purchase. Dave was already on the way to the hospital in the ambulance. No other news.

What followed was a drilling of questions by the attending police officers regarding contact information and relationships. Rightly so! They were leaving no stone unturned. They made it very clear that I was not to contact Dave's wife. That would be their job. They were concerned that Dave's wife worked in a place an hour out of town. It was their directive she should not be made aware of what happened until she arrived home or else be driven home by a police officer. Why? She might become a danger to herself or others on the road due to having a major distraction.

An unforgettable afternoon

I headed to the hospital with Dave's personal administrative assistant, who, I might add, had been working part-time for me over the previous year. The two of us arrived at the hospital, fully anticipating to be led to where the doctors were working on Dave. Finally, the attending police officer arrived and led us through locked doors in the emergency department of the hospital.

Oh, oh! There's a Kleenex box . . .

I knew it. As soon as I saw the small room he was directing us to, furnished with only a couch and a box of Kleenex, it quickly sank in, and my heart sank as well. It wasn't until the officer began "I'm very, very sorry but . . ." that our assistant became aware of the full extent of the horror. Dave had succumbed to a major heart attack. This afternoon was not just poignant. It was another day from hell.

I phoned our branch manager, knowing the police were diligently working on getting in contact with Dave's wife. He quickly arrived, and the three of us discussed future plans and how we could best be of help to Dave's wife when she arrived. The rest of the afternoon remains a complete blur.

The only comic relief, if I can call it that, came from the hospital chaplain. Dave's wife had asked for a final prayer at the hospital, and the minister, seemingly taking forever, finally arrived at the hospital. There may not be an exact protocol they are supposed to take, but I believe promptness should be part of that protocol. After what seemed well over an hour later, he finally arrived. He started in with a final prayer for Dave.

God bless Doug?

It was four or five times he used the name Doug in the prayer before our branch manager interrupted in a quiet, tactful, and forceful way: "His name is DAVE, not Doug!"

There was dead silence, if I can call it that. Major faux pas! He started over. Little did the chaplain realize he would provide a bit of comic relief and would be written about later in a book on personal finance. Maybe St. Peter at the gate will say, "Come on in, Doug, your name is right here on the list!" When I said "major faux pas," I meant just that. Dave would be busting a gut, laughing. I knew him well.

"All's well that ends well." That line is Shakespeare, isn't it? My English teacher would be proud.

Terms of endearment

I have one last comment before I move on. This actually happened. Dave was always calling me shithead. I did not mind. To me it was a term of endearment. It's a guy thing. For all my life, I had never been hit by seagull bombing its excrement. Never! Quite a life accomplishment, wouldn't you say?

The day of Dave's funeral and an hour before we were to be there, I stopped into McDonald's for a coffee. I wanted to read the paper as a bit of a distraction, have a coffee, and let my emotions settle. I think you see it coming. There in the parking lot, whammo! Some damn seagull got me, right on the shoulder, but not the head. I looked up and said, "You missed, Dave! But only by a foot." Is that not an omen, or what? I think Dave was hammering home what he said to me earlier.

So what?

Do you not see the irony in the statement "Anything can happen anytime"? The fact is, when tragedy strikes, it is always the other guy, right? It is most of the time, but not always. The fact is, no one has any kind of guarantee of living eighty-five years. You might be dead tomorrow. I really do not like talking about morbidity, but don't forget what I said about the ostrich. Tragedy can and does strike. It could be far worse than just a seagull bombing your shoulder. Just look at what happened to Dave. He was fifty-six years of age and taken out. Bang!

I said I was going to sell the sizzle and not the steak, so here it is: *peace of mind*. You want it? It can be yours. You really need to speak to your financial advisor because that is another thing he or she sells. How? It is called estate planning. What does that involve?

I have already extolled the virtues of speaking with your lawyer about having a last will and testament and powers of attorney prepared for yourself. Otherwise, the government will decide for you how your hard-earned assets will be distributed or if you become incapacitated, medical decisions may be stalled. "Anything can happen anytime!" You saw what happened to Dave.

Think about the week after you die. How will your loved ones be treated? How will your executor fare? How will your spouse and kids fare? Have you appointed a guardian for your minor kids should both you and your wife be tragically taken at the same time?

Anything can happen anytime!

If you have a will, wonderful, but ask yourself these questions: Does your executor have the full picture? What about passwords on your computer? What about subscriptions that may need cancelling? What about heirlooms you may have hidden away? Dead people don't speak, I might remind you!

I continue: Who is your lawyer? Do you have an accountant or someone that prepares your taxes for you? What are their phone numbers? A final tax filing will have to be done by your executor, I might add. Who is your financial advisor, or did you even have one? I would like the phone number, please! Your executor may be headed for one real nightmare. The nightmare that you left! All because you made the mistake of surmising, "It won't happen to me! I'll write some stuff down someday, but not yet. It won't happen just quite yet!" What is the cost of your being wrong? There is an answer. If you have a financial advisor worth a pinch of salt, he or she would have been raising these issues with you.

I have to make one more plug for my hero Dave. Shortly after he came to our office, he organized and outsourced a printing source and prepared an estate record keeper, as well as a booklet called "The Role of an Executor: What You Need to Know." (Most of the work was done by our administrative assistant, but I don't want accolades to inflate her ego!)

Estate information can now be organized in an accordion folder complete with tabs that are customizable. Here in bullet form are items you need to catalogue:

- The name and address of your executor

- Your last will and testament

- Powers of attorney

- The name and address of your lawyer, accountant, or whoever has been preparing your taxes in the past

- Any business contracts

- Business insurance

- Life insurance

- Car insurance

- Home insurance

- Loans and liabilities

- Bank account statements, including account numbers

- Investment information (has your advisor done a net worth statement for you?)

- Stock and bonds you may own

- GICs

- Mutual funds—both registered plans as well as nonregistered

This list is in no way complete. It is specific to your situation. Believe me, this is the kind of stuff that will make you a hero in the eyes of your executor. Dave had it together, and I am enjoying discussing these items with clients in their estate planning.

The sizzle here is peace of mind. I challenge you to think about this. If you died tomorrow, what kind of time would your executor have in settling your estate? Either your executor will have an easy time or a difficult time settling your affairs. I think we really do need to answer this question, and if you have already taken care of this, you should already have peace of mind in this regard.

I once counseled an elderly couple that proudly announced that all three of their adult children were named in their will as joint executors. Not joint and several, just joint—which meant all three of their adult children would have to sign every legal document to settle the estate. After inquiring about their location, capacity, and more importantly, about how they got along with each other, I discovered a major problem. One of the three clearly was a black sheep. There had been a history of poor communication because of familial disharmony.

I exclaimed, "Houston, we have a problem!" I advised them that the first thing they should do when they left my office was to make an appointment with their lawyer to choose one of their adult children as executor. The decision should be based entirely upon age, capacity, availability, and most important of all, trust.

When you designate only one of your adult children as executor, *it does not mean you love any of the others less than the one you choose.* I have seen the unfortunate problems that can happen between joint executors when Mom and Dad are no longer around to referee and no threat of being taken off the beneficiary list exists. All hell can break loose over "stuff." It is so sad but true.

Believe me, anything can happen anytime.

Do you want that peace of mind, or don't you? You may have less time than you think. Talk to your advisor. Sizzle.

Chapter Ten

WHAT REALLY COUNTS?

Twenty-eight years old and I'm lying flat on my back looking up at fluorescent lights. One long week, I might add. I know where I am situated; it is just that I don't remember *why I am here or how I got here* at Mississauga General Hospital. They told me something to the effect that I had just been in a major car accident. I vaguely remember being quickly wheeled down the hallway to the emergency room on the gurney, all the while someone asking what my wife's name was. "I'm not married!" I protested. The nurse assured me that I was since I had a wedding ring on my finger. I may have been semicomatose, but I wasn't stupid. "Please don't tell her I didn't remember, or she'll finish me off!"

Kinetic energy

This was a close brush with death. This major car accident had not only totalled the car, it almost totalled me. The guy with the sickle called the Grim Reaper came close, calling my name. It is funny how these moments can bring your life into focus in a big hurry. Thoughts not familiar to a twenty-eight-year-old crept through my mind: *I almost died! I almost didn't have the joy of seeing a child of my own born. I am too young to die! I could have broken my wife's heart.* I almost cried. Perhaps I did as it has been many years since the accident occurred, and my memory is not quite that good.

Many thoughts flooded my mind that week in the hospital with one sole focus: if I almost died, then what? Is there really life after death? Or is it how Porky Pig always closed Bugs Bunny cartoons: "Abba-dabba-dah . . . That's all folks!" What do I really want with my life? What must I do so that at the end of the road I will have no regrets? I would much rather reach that point in my life with a Fred Flintstone exclamation: "Yaba-daba-dooo!"

Will people I care about even care how I have lived my life? What would be said of me at my funeral? Does it really matter? Wait a minute! *I almost did* make it to the end of my road. So then, do I have any regrets right now? Do I have any outstanding social IOUs? What really counts? You may have already guessed this. *I formulated Ozzie Causey's reflection on the meaning of his life from that hospital bed.* Go back and check chapter 2 if you missed it or have forgotten. I find meaning in every word.

Electric energy

This was not the only incident in my life like this. One day I was almost electrocuted while standing in a puddle of water, nine hundred feet underground in a mine. A mine official had assured me an electrical panel was locked out at the source of its power in another location with his own personal lock on the switch. While preparing to jump down off a flat belt conveyor, I grabbed on to some structural steel supporting the electrical panel and quickly found out otherwise.

Six seconds of pure shock, actual and figurative. My life flashed before me. In those six excruciating seconds, I screamed for help. No one wanted to touch me; everyone had a reasonable fear of getting the shock themselves. The muscles in my hand, my one arm, and one leg completely froze. I could not let go, despite my most valiant effort. I could move my other arm, and a little angel whispered in my ear, "Rolf, you can move your other arm, so use it!" With that word of encouragement, I used the other arm and hit the frozen one off the structural steel.

Hey, I'm famous!

One day a few years later while eating pizza, I learned that I had through this accident become an incident of notation in the mining safety journals. No, I am not joking. These journals are distributed across the province to all mining safety captains upon any incident involving mining safety. As it turned out, the owner of the pizza parlor was a retired mining safety captain. He recited accurate details of the incident that convinced me I definitely was the man he spoke of in his story. Thanks, but I would rather not have had such notoriety. Again, the Grim Reaper turned away.

The gravity of gravity

You may be starting to think I am a cat with nine lives. Sorry, I am not even a feline fan; I'm allergic to their dander. In this third brush with death, I will only mention a few details. I had a fall off a shuttle conveyor that was being constructed for a large mill, and I was supervising the installation of equipment. I had sold this product to the equipment manufacturer of the conveyor and was assisting with installation of the equipment.

The fall would not have been so much a problem. However, there was a one-thousand-pound box of gear assembly following close behind! I sprung away as I fell, knowing full well the box could easily crush my legs. Despite my calculated backward spring from my starting point, my movements would not have bidden well in a diving competition. The landing was rough. I thank God the box landed away from me. My tailbone still bothers me twenty years later.

So what! So what?

May I take a stroll back to "Anything can happen anytime"? The death of a loved one or a close brush with death yourself can easily make you wax nostalgic. Is that not a good thing? We only have one kick at the can in life, so should it not be a touchdown, if not a field goal?

The Wizard of Cause certainly thought so. I have had plenty of time to reflect and plenty of impetus to do so.

Turning point

So here is my point of inflection. What about you? Have you given it much thought? Or will it take a close call for you or the death of someone you really care for before you give it any thought? What really counts for you? Everyone leaves footprints in the sand as we live, whether we think about it or not. That includes you, my friend.

The cycle of life

As we approach retirement years, the thought of what will we do to keep ourselves occupied and happy during those years comes into focus. For some planning even further ahead, the thought of what about what happens to their family after their own demise comes into play, something called estate planning.

For many years as people plan for their future, they tend to focus most of their energy toward wealth accumulation alone. "Will I have enough funds to do the kinds of things I want to do?" asks the client. The advisor then asks the client to be more specific as to what kind of things the client wishes to do. "I'm not quite sure, but I like playing golf." The real question is what will be your full needs, not just your perceived ones. Again, this could very well be another case of truth versus opinion. What is the rest of the story? What are needs you may have missed? What will all your needs be in retirement? These are important questions for you!

"This retirement thing isn't all it's cracked up to be!"

We were having lunch, discussing matters of business, when my client surprised me with this statement. He humored me with a follow-up retort: "The only thing golden about the golden years is your urine." He and his wife had retired a few years previous, with full intention of golfing their way into the sunset of their life. They moved to a remote location, complete with a small lake and a private golf course adjacent to their new home. His statement startled me as clearly his total needs were not being met. It wasn't an issue of wealth accumulation; it was the effect of seclusion upon their lives they had not accounted for in their planning. They were accustomed to more activities in their previous community. Clearly, they needed more activities to satisfy their needs.

Maslow's hierarchy of needs

Through several courses I have taken in years gone by, our dear psychologist friend Dr. Abraham Maslow and his pyramid representing the universal needs of humanity were discussed at great length. Although I enrolled in general sciences at the University of Alberta, a few social elective courses were required to round out our education. I recall a buddy of mine saying, "Take sociology! The classes are loaded with girls!" Other than Maslow, the only memory I have of Sociology 101 is that including myself, there were only three guys in the class. All the rest were not, and I didn't mind one bit. It is a wonder I even remember Dr. Maslow and his pyramid.

Just the basics

At the bottom of the pyramid were basic needs we all have, which are physiological in nature. Things like food, shelter, sleep, and sex get memorable mention. If you were to fulfill only one of the five levels of needs, choose this one. This would be a level you could call just the basics. Without addressing this level, you are not going to be a happy camper. You need to eat, among a few other basic items.

Safety

The next level concerns itself with your security or safety. Things like a home security system, which I did not purchase until after the break-and-enter at my residence. Worrying about job layoffs or being fired would also be considered to be part of this level. This is the level poor Ozzie Causey was dealing with that night he did not sleep well. The fear of not having sufficient resources would also fit into this level. Many Canadians have not investigated what level Canada Pension Plan will be for them or Old Age Security. Remember, only half of Canadians have any kind of pension plan at all. The government won't let me starve, right? You would have to first define your meaning of the word *starve*. We will briefly discuss these government plans in the next chapter.

People who need people

Further up the pyramid, occupying a smaller area is one of belonging: feeling that you are loved or wanted. From what I remember of the class, the farther up the pyramid you go, the more refined these needs become. The artist and singer Barbra Streisand so eloquently expressed this issue in her song "People Who Need People." No man is an island. We were never designed that way. We are social beings.

Am I good, or what?

The next level higher, nearest the peak level, is how you view yourself: your self-esteem. This would be what you see when you look in the mirror. Are you happy with what you see? I guess all that bouncing on Mom's knee did me a bit of good because another story comes to mind: "Mirror, mirror on the wall, who's the fairest of them all?" Better yet, what do you see when you are lying in a hospital bed, reviewing your life? We are not talking about an inflated ego. The world has too many of these types who seem to be full of themselves. We are talking about having a healthy self-respect.

Self-actualization

Last but certainly not least is the pinnacle level of needs located at the very top of the pyramid. This level is what Dr. Maslow calls self-actualization. That would include meaningful things in life, such as your authenticity, creativity, and sense of fulfillment. Many people live their lives in such a way that most of their needs are addressed, but this top level requires fine-tuning. Unfortunately, many people miss considering this level of need in their life management.

Why have I included this construct in this chapter? Once again, from countless meetings with people projecting their future needs, I believe this construct is a very good way to look at and prepare for your own future needs. This kind of preparation is not only a question of "Will you have enough money?" Do not forget about Dr. Maslow and self-actualization. Your days of retirement will be far more than trips to the bank and the grocery store if you are to fulfill your needs. That is, if you wish to have meaning in your retirement. That is, if you want that Fred Flintstone exuberance with your life. Wouldn't you like to be in such a state of exuberance with your life you can't help shouting "Yabba-dabba-doo"?

Know thyself!

The great philosopher Socrates stated words that have lasted many hundreds of years, and I might guess the words have lasted that long because the truth contained therein is plain and simple. This is his short, remarkable phrase: "Know thyself!" How intelligent and insightful that is! There are people that really have not taken a very good look at themselves in the mirror when projecting what their full needs are today, let alone in the future.

I am not sure if the story is true or not, but I think it carries some food for thought. The story I heard was of a gentleman and his wife who decided they wished to sail into retirement with a sailboat out at the coast. These people had visited the east coast on numerous occasions but had never lived there. They had only done some recreational sailing on various lakes but never on seawater. They were prepared to take many navigational and sailing courses available, and this for them was a romantic perception of their retirement. This turned out to be a bad decision as they discovered after purchasing the vessel that she suffered from seasickness. If any swells of any significance developed on the sea, it would affect her in ways we will not describe here.

Antinausea pills were of not much use, and they soon began to realize their dream would not come to fruition. Their dream vessel went up for sale.

Objectives

One of the constructs taught to advisors is a specific process of providing financial advice. The first step is to determine the client's goal. You do not know where you are going unless your destination has been chosen. This goal may be as specific as you like, but remember, the less specific you make the goal, the more difficult it is to measure and monitor progress.

Gathering data

The second step involves gathering data. This would be the step of discovering many financial details from the client. It may involve making a net worth statement. To get to this number, we first have to calculate your *net liquid assets*. This includes assets that are fairly easy to convert to cash, such as bank deposits, investments such as stocks, bonds, GICs, or mutual funds. To that sum you would also include registered assets within your RSP or RIF, whether contributed by yourself or your employer in a locked-in plan. From this sum you would deduct any loans outstanding, such as student loans, investment loans, and any credit card balances outstanding. This resulting figure would be your net liquid assets.

The next calculation would be to find your *net fixed assets*, which are more difficult to sell and convert to cash. This would include items like your principal residence, any rental property you might own, or other real estate, such as a summer cottage. In this sum you would also include major items of personal-use property, such as an automobile (the current market value, not what you purchased it for!) and major heirlooms of significant value, such as works of art or a grand piano, for example. From this total, you must deduct your mortgage outstanding, the principal outstanding on your car loan, and personal bank loans, such as the balance outstanding on a home equity line of credit. This number will result in your net fixed assets. Whew! This seems like a bunch of calculation! One more calculation and you will come to the point of the exercise, finding your net worth at that point of time in your life.

Your financial net worth

Simply take the two numbers you came to: the net liquid assets and the net fixed assets, add them together, and this number becomes a snapshot of where you are at this point in time. This number is called your net worth and quantifies where you are financially. It is a good point of reference to challenge you from year to year, and to ask two very good questions: "What are we doing right?" and "What are we doing wrong?"

Other items of discussion when gathering data would include all sources of income and all debts you currently have. Yes, that hidden line of credit is important to get the whole picture. You wouldn't hide symptoms from your doctor and jeopardize your health, would you? It is the same kind of folly hiding these negative items from your financial advisor if you want a true assessment of your financial picture. Items such as financial assistance for your child going to university or care of elderly parents are also of major financial concern. Do you believe you have a chance for promotion at work, or is that a stretch beyond your belief? These are the kinds of questions that financial advisors should be asking in the collection of data specific to your situation.

Strategy

I promised in the first sentence in this book I would be selling sizzle more than the steak, and I will keep this section short. Suffice it to say there many books on the shelf with wonderful strategies on getting from where you are now to where you would like to be. I am going to talk more about the journey and the destination. Strategy is what financial advisors do for a living, and this is a discussion you need to have with your advisor.

Implementation

We already spoke of a client with a plan but no plan to change financial behavior to meet the goals set out in the plan. Of what use is the plan? It is like looking in the mirror and immediately forgetting what you saw. Would you not agree this is useless? I have already spoken about using automated systems to keep you on track, such as preauthorized checking plans (PACs). There are however, some advisors that believe everyone must be on a strict budget and monitor every dime they spend.

As I told you earlier, I have been in sales for many years and am also opinionated. I have never once worked from a personal budget. I do not believe I am lazy for not doing so either. We are not focusing here on either my ability or attitude. The problem here for me is one of aptitude for detailed budgeting. That just isn't me.

It has been my experience that what is important in our family life is A > B. Our family net income is greater than our net expenses. How do I accomplish this automatically? We pay ourselves first! (Please refer to David Chilton—buy his books if you have not already done so.) This for our family is facilitated by way of a PAC (refer back to the middle of chapter 5). My wife and I make mini decisions on family purchases based on what remains in our joint bank account. That is, as long as we have net savings, by comparison the rest does not matter (refer back to chapter 4).

The system works well for us, and my wife and I are on the same page. Again, the system is simple and also works automatically. Does this require effective communication? Absolutely! In my opinion, that is what successful marriage is about: being on the same page. I am a strong believer of joint bank accounts for spouses, with no hidden secrets. These accounts are registered as joint trust with rights of survivorship. In case something happened to either one of us, such as incapacity or death, the funds are outside of our estate, fully liquid, and free from that other tax called probate.

Monitoring

Some clients believe monitoring their portfolio is completely up to the advisor. I believe dialogue is a two-way street, and if you do not understand something on your statement, call your advisor and initiate dialogue on your concern! You need to know why you own what you own, and if it is underperforming assets in the same class, is there a good reason for it? What are the prospects for that investment on a go-forward basis? The only monitoring the clients may be implementing themselves is comparing the bottom line from the last statement to the current one. Clearly, there is more to it than that.

I have one last comment about the process of financial advice. It is a process. Once these five steps are completed, you may soon find yourself back at step 1. Your financial situation may change. The results of the expected rate of return you assumed in your strategy may not come to fruition. Health issues may strike, and you find yourself in an entirely different scenario. Herein is the value of working with a financial advisor.

I love my job.

Chapter Eleven

Out of the Fry Pan

Having a rough day?

Ever had a rough day like the day Ozzie Causey lost his job? Suddenly the world seems to be crumbling about you. Nothing seems to be going right. The issue at hand usually centers on something not going the way you had hoped or planned. One day the birds are singing, the sun is shining, and life seems as if it couldn't get much better. Suddenly, something strikes far worse than a seagull letting loose on your shoulder. Someone you love dies or is hurt.

Out of the blue your supervisor speaks those same words Ozzie heard: "You are fired!" Your supervisor may dress up the words to make it seem *management is being ever so considerate*, such as "I don't think you really want to work here." The effect is still the same. You now have no job. You just lost the main source of your family income, if not all of it. We have already spoken of the fact that anything can happen to anyone, and you just might happen to become the star of the show.

There seems to be such a stigma assigned to getting fired. The question always remains: "Where did I do wrong?" Oh, there are words you can use to dress it up when explaining it to family and friends to make it sound better. "I was part of a downsizing. There was a reorganizing of the corporate structure, and I became part of the shuffle out the door. I never had any backing from my supervisor from the start. I was not suited to their change in mission. It was a poisoned environment, and I just didn't fit in." The list goes on, but there are multiple ways to dress up the reality and make it more palatable. The fact remains, you are out of an income until you find another paying job. Hopefully, it would be well suited to your skills, aptitude, and ability. Happiness in your work should be considered a need, would you not agree?

Over thirty years ago I was taking a walk in the rain, after receiving in the mail my university transcript revealing my total ineptitude with second-year calculus. It had been a struggle in first year, and now it was much, much worse. It hit me like a ton of bricks. I had put every ounce of energy I could into getting that iron ring around my baby finger. I wanted desperately to become a civil engineer. I now was faced with a very serious fact. It would never happen.

Somewhere over the rainbow

Why am I dredging up personal calamity from way back? Am I bitter? No, not at all! In fact, my feelings are quite contrary. I can truthfully say it charted me into a course more suited to my aptitude. I also believe one of the greatest gifts in life is to be happy with your line of work. Work then becomes a hobby, not a chore. I was just too stubborn to recognize truth. At that moment, it seemed to me like the end of the world. Again, it was a case of truth versus my stubborn opinion. I didn't have the eyes to see. When we face obstacles in our life, it often obscures opportunity existing just beyond the obstacle. The same rings true in personal finance. We need to look beyond the obstacle that is likely obscuring a golden opportunity. A big part of escaping that stubborn opinion would be to overcome it with a different attitude: that is, attitude with a capital A.

There's got to be something good in there

Parents of twins, a boy and a girl, were amazed how different in temperament the two were. As the children grew, they noticed that no matter what they did, the girl was the eternal optimist, and the boy was exactly opposite, pessimistic in everything that was said or done. Trying to even their temperaments, they took them to a psychologist for repair.

After observing the two for the better part of an hour, the assessment came from the psychologist. He said, "Next Christmas give the best gifts you can imagine to your son, the pessimist. Make sure you also give your daughter, the optimist, a gift or two, but make the gifts as untenable as you can imagine. Be creative!" That should even the two out.

Christmas arrived, and the results they achieved were not as expected. The pessimist son was very upset and agitated: "My train isn't the model I wanted, and it will probably break anyway. I didn't want a bike either! This is the worst Christmas ever! Santa screwed up royally!"

They went outside to see the results with their daughter, the optimist. They had only bought her an old plastic shovel that didn't even have a pail, and got very creative with the second gift: a pile of manure. That's right, a pile of manure on the driveway, delivered right off the farm. They had reasoned by spring the pile would be ready to dig into the flower and vegetable garden. That's what the psychologist recommended! He had told them to be creative, and creative they certainly were!

To their surprise, their daughter, the optimist, was as happy as a lark, singing away, all the while digging with great determination in the pile. When they asked what she was doing, she replied, "Gee, Santa is just awesome! There's got to be a pony in there somewhere!"

The point I make again is, attitude has a great deal to do with your ultimate direction. It definitely affects choices you make, which develop into habits.

Excuses, excuses

I do not know your financial state. You may have lost your source of income due to "a change in company mission." You may have bitten hard on easy money coming from a home equity line of credit, and the interest charged is now starting to snowball. You may be having the credit card blues in January after a memorable Christmas season. You may have a well-rehearsed multitude of excuses: "I only live once! My family now has Caribbean memories that can never be taken away. If George down the street can afford a new car, then so can we! I had to buy a four-bedroom house—we have three kids!"

There's a white elephant in the room

You may be in more danger yet, falling behind in mortgage payments and worrying about a bailiff coming to change locks on your home. Or you may have missed a couple of car payments and you worry some nights the sound of a motor running in your driveway is from a repossession expert. Your phone may be ringing off the hook from creditors, and you are very thankful for call display. You may be facing something far worse: personal bankruptcy. Just how did this white elephant get in my room? It may be in your room and you don't even realize it. Worse yet, you may well realize its presence, but it is deliberately being ignored: "I'll deal with it later!"

Even though I don't know your financial state, if you have a white elephant in the room, I suspect that I can piece together how it got there. Go back to the Lake of Two Rivers and examine your income versus your lifestyle. I would place a strong bet your river draining the lake has been bigger than the one filling it, and for quite some time. You may be as stubborn as my civil engineering dream—stubborn in assessing your wants versus actual needs. Reality check!

You are convinced your assessment of your financial state is solid truth. But some little angel on your shoulder is whispering: "Something is just not quite right and needs fixing." Keeping up with the Joneses has crept into your life, and you did not realize it. Your wants have been deliberately categorized as absolute needs. Oh, that cool and drool is not just an attitude. It is a disease, and it is contagious. Don't forget your curiosity. It just may spark a realization of truth, and your opinion may not be congruent with that truth.

A temporary shift from sizzle to steak

I know, I promised from the outset I would focus in this book mostly on your benefits, and I believe, for the most part, I have been true to that goal. I have a strong belief that a focus on benefit is the most likely way to cause a change in behavior. If not an actual change of behavior, at least it would cause someone to be willing to at least examine their habits. There are many people out there who actually do have a white elephant in the room and don't know what to do about it.

I wish to briefly summarize my thoughts regarding those burdened with debt and share my most basic financial philosophy. I realize this summary deals more with "What should I do?" more than "Why should I do it?" I just don't want you as a reader believing I am willing to ignore elephants in the room.

1. Live within your means. If you haven't understood me yet, this should be at the top of your agenda.

2. Get out of debt as soon as possible. The banks understand human behavior and tend to capitalize on it. They know the "cool and drool" disease. The interest you pay is the stream into their lake, not yours. Many times a client wishes to understand which is of more advantage to them: pay down debt or invest. Often it is better to pay down the debt, but it truly depends on your financial situation, and that is why you need a financial advisor.

3. Be extremely careful about borrowing. A millionaire is not one who necessarily has a million dollars in the bank. Net worth, as we discovered, is net liquid assets plus net fixed assets. The word *net* means you have accounted for things you owe. Paying down debt absolutely increases your net worth, regardless of market movements. Borrowing to invest, or leverage, is a high-risk strategy that may work for you, but it may not as well, mostly depending on future market movements. However, leverage magnifies both the upside and the downside. If the market turns south, you are still responsible for the loan, and you may even receive a call for more money to deposit to your account to protect investments that have turned south in a

way you never expected. Leverage should never be entered in without full understanding, full capacity to handle that risk, and full disclosure. Again, consult a financial advisor before ever borrowing to invest.

4. If you need help, ask for some! I am speaking mostly in the realm of advice, but realize there may be a time when you just can't make it on your own. There may come a time when even your basic needs cannot be met by your sources of income. Beware: borrowing from family has high social risk. The gray area of payment back to family versus "it was meant as a gift" is often later argued, and much strife can be caused over this dangerous activity.

5. Seek an opinion beyond yourself. This gets back to my Wizard of Cause that pointed out that everyone has areas in which they would profit from professional help. This may be advice from a financial advisor, or it may be someone in business, who likely will be charging for this service. Everyone must make a living. Beware of hot stock tips from friends at social parties. It is only the ones that were winners that are bragged about. The losers are kept quiet and hidden in the closet.

6. Diversify your investments. There are times when certain asset classes come into favor, depending on the economic cycle. There are some that have all their equity built into a single business. You have heard "Don't put all your eggs in one basket." If that one basket falls, all the eggs are in jeopardy.

7. Stay true to your strategy. The sinusoidal curve representing investor sentiment rings out one truth: your emotions should play no role in your investment strategy. If you follow your emotions, you definitely will not have the control to buy low and sell high. People tend to use their rearview mirror when it comes to buying or selling investments.

These few points outline a basic financial philosophy I adopted over the years, and certainly, these are in no way comprehensive advice to you or a strategy. Financial advice is quite personal and is also custom work that needs to be specific to your objectives. An appropriate strategy can only be developed after considerable discussion around your specific financial situation. Again, you should speak to your advisor and discuss these goals and strategies.

Row, row, row your boat

How many of you have been to a summer camp? What is a camp without the campfire and a good singsong to go along? My mouth is starting to water thinking about those melt-in-your-mouth s'mores. I was told the name came from someone slurring with a mouthful, "I want s'more!" Toasted marshmallows and melting chocolate, all between two honey graham crackers—what could be better to go with that than a good round of "Row, Row, Row Your Boat" and a crackling fire? It would surprise me if you don't know the lyrics. It's the type of song that if you start in midstream (forgive me for using another water term), the differing parts start to harmonize in a lovely way. It has a very catchy tune. The lyrics are likely emblazoned in your memory. They certainly are in mine.

Actually, I've had a few years to think about it. Nice song, but I now hate the lyrics. Why? The next line is "Merrily, merrily, merrily, merrily, life is but a dream!" Now what is that supposed to imply? Again, I think there's allegory. There are far too many people in this world that do not give a second glance to charity, empathy for others, or even much thought about what kind of a life they are choosing. They just float along like a cork happily down the stream, not even thinking there just might be a rudder or tiller that could land them in a preferable spot should they decide to do something about it.

Important issues

I think the lyrics of this song are similar in sentiment to yet another well-known song: "Que será, será, whatever will be, will be!" Floating along where the current takes you, or leaving your destination all to chance (whatever will be, will be) is not my idea of life management skills, let alone quality management of personal finances. There are many choices to be made along the way! The real question is written in yet another song: "Which way you going, Billy?"

These artists have a way of putting their finger on some very important issues and questions. You really should ask yourself these kinds of questions. Know thyself! No, my friend, the simple plain truth is, *life is not a dream.* Does that not make you curious? It should. You are at a higher-stakes table than you may realize. Truth versus opinion! It is for real, and you do have choices that factor in greatly your destination. You are not a cork. As we touched on earlier, it is not an individual financial choice you make but a choice of choices. It is your continued financial habits that matter. Your financial destination depends upon them.

Planning for a trip

Planning activities, such as taking a vacation trip, takes a great deal of preparation. First, there are details such as where the destination is and what you will do when you get there. How long will you be staying? How far is it from here to there? Do you know the way by heart, or will you need to refer to a map? Have you ever even been there before, or do you know of someone who has told you about the place you intend to visit?

Automobile associations are a great assistance

Here is a plug for membership in an automobile association. These kinds of associations provide information that is very useful. As a member of the Canadian Automobile Association (CAA), for many years we have relied on them for this kind of information. They provided us by request a custom triptych that is very useful. These kinds of triptychs indicate not only how to get there but also what you might expect along your way, like points of interest, for example. Included in the customized map are details such as mileage or kilometers between points along the way, estimated time that it will take between various points, and total travel time. It even helps you decide which route is best to travel. They may show more than one route—one showing the most scenic route, and another the quickest, most economic route you would find. Have you checked for road reports? These details are often included. Is there any road construction you need to worry about? What will be required of you along the way there?

There is a myriad of other questions needing to be asked. Personal items of clothing, personal hygiene, sports equipment, or possibly reading material during leisure time at your destination, such as a book on personal finance. (Just kidding.) Will you be stopping for a picnic lunch on the side of the road, or will that even be necessary? What essentials will you need along the way? If the weather report is good, will you need your sunglasses? You may be camping, which opens a whole new area of concerns for cooking, shelter, outdoor clothing, and don't forget the mosquito repellent! Or the suntan lotion!

Okay, once again, I beat it to death. I think you get the picture. Taking a vacation by car is not as simple as we might first guess. What reminds us of the need to take inventory is when you recall one or two items you missed but not until you are an hour down the road. "Sorry, honey, it is too late to turn back now!"

There's more allegory here

We have seen choosing a road trip takes a great deal of planning and organization if it is to be a pleasurable experience. This is very similar to a trip we are all taking, the experience of life itself. Whether we choose to or not, if you are alive and well, you are heading to a destination. Chosen or not, but you are heading in that direction. Have you first taken any kind of inventory?

The destination spoken of here is where you either choose not to work, or the decision is made for you. That destination may well be ten, twenty, or even thirty years away, but it may be much closer than your expectation.

Your health may hold until your date of death, and you may choose continuing working, especially if you are enjoying what you are doing and the work is not physically taxing. Eventually, there may come something forcing your hand, such as old age or incapacity caused by an accidental injury.

A plain, simple truth our friend Ozzie Causey understood was his need for income. He innately knew that income was required to provide for basic needs for himself and his family. They were depending on him. His needs were far more than just clothing, food, and shelter. He and his family had other needs requiring tending to as well.

Just like preparing for a road trip, you need to be smart about your future. You truly need to take an inventory of all your future needs and how those needs will be met. Many Canadians have no idea what level of support they can expect to attain from the government. Fortunately, Canada Pension Plan is indexed to inflation, as well as Old Age Security, but not all Canadians receive the full benefit. I would strongly advise you to search out information on these benefits from the government website http://www.cra-arc.gc.ca.

Pillars in retirement on which you may or may not be able to rely:

A. Government plans such as Canada Pension Plan and Old Age Security. Some people will also be able to rely on Guaranteed Income Supplement. Some of these benefits are income tested (you won't be eligible if your income is too high), and yes, there is a 15 percent clawback on Old Age Security if your income exceeds a level they specify. Don't forget these government plans must be applied for!

I recently heard of a ninety-three-year-old whose relatives had only recently started working on a Power of Attorney for her. They discovered she had never applied for either Old Age Security or Canada Pension Plan. This meant twenty-eight years of benefits were not claimed, and her only source of income was from the rent received by sharing her condo with another person. Government rules would only allow them to reclaim one of those twenty-eight years. It almost sounds like the government took lessons from the banks; would it not seem that way?

While on the subject, don't forget that the Canada Pension Plan Death Benefit must also be applied for! This benefit pays up to $2,500 upon death. Statistically, this benefit is only claimed in half of the cases! Be very sure to take advantage of this. Many funeral homes are now providing guidance in this field, but make sure you apply for it on behalf of any loved one passed.

B. Pensions. Defined benefit pension plans are becoming very scarce as these programs must be fully funded by the company providing them to meet their actuarial determined future obligations to pensioners. More common plans are defined contribution plans that determine how much may be contributed by the employee and to what level the company will match those contributions. In any case, statistics show that only half of working Canadians have any type of pension plan at all.

C. Private holdings. This would be the area that is most dangerous to neglect. If you do not take heed like the squirrels on this one, you may well be shooting yourself in the foot! The Registered Retirement Savings Plan and Registered Retirement Income Funds are programs designed to assist you to accumulate retirement funds and liquidate these holdings in an efficient manner.

D. A business that you plan to sell or second properties. These are areas where you may or may not require outside professional help in liquidating in a timely fashion. Life insurance may greatly assist you in succession planning for your business interests.

E. Whole life insurance policies. Permanent insurance is designed to be utilized over the whole life of the annuitant. These permanent policies tend to have higher premiums in the beginning as compared to term life policies with similar face-value death benefit. However, as years advance, the value of permanent insurance becomes realized, particularly regarding estate planning.

There is a great benefit to those who have participated in this kind of insurance, taking risk off the table for the client; this is accomplished through contractual obligations the insurance company takes on in return for premiums paid by the client.

This chapter has been challenging for me, placing these ideas on paper. Strategy is most often tailored to specific client objectives; I have found my challenge to be greatest in making these suggestions generic. I hope that I have awakened your curiosity to that simple question "What if?" Financial advisors deal with a multiplicity of client situations, and each case must be dealt with in custom fashion.

It is also my hope you are not sharing your room with a white elephant. If you are, I will have accomplished my goal if I have convinced you to eat that elephant, one bite at a time.

Chapter Twelve

UP THE CHIMNEY

It was 1:30 a.m., late in November 1999, when the doorbell rang. Both my wife and I were startled as we had just gone to bed twenty minutes earlier after a very intense day. The day had been very busy with preparations as the Wizard of Cause had died in our presence at the hospital less than twenty-four hours earlier. The preparations were for a service of celebration of his life as he deserved nothing but the best.

A doorbell and a seagull

But what was this? I hurried down the stairs only to find no one at the door. I will not give an explanation here because I cannot. Both I and my wife will attest to the fact the doorbell rang. In the same way, I cannot explain getting bombed by a seagull one hour before the funeral of a close friend that always called me shithead. Were these just coincidences? Perhaps, but not in my mind! I care to dream, and I care to read my own interpretation into it. There is more to life than what can be measured in a test tube and a Bunsen burner. Let's leave it at that. What I wish to point out in this final chapter is the power of dreaming. Do not forget your curiosity. It is more powerful than you might think.

Curiosity

From the outset of this book, we began showing how curiosity is essential for the advancement of knowledge and spoke of plain, simple truth. Investing involves both risk and potential return and by nature requires capital placed at some kind of risk. We also noted that education is no guarantee of investment success. There are plenty of people out there with a big hat but no cattle and delight in flaunting the hat. We also saw that opinions may not necessarily line up with truth, simply because they may not be seeing the entire picture. Perhaps they have been denying their own curiosity for whatever reason.

Wisdom that keeps giving

In chapter 2 we told a parable starring our friend Ozzie, who seemed to play all his cards right but ran into bad luck. Fortunately, he realized his source of happiness in life was to be found in something other than things. He also recognized his need for continuing income to cover continuing expenses. We saw the importance of wisdom passed down from one generation to the next by the Wizard of Cause.

Plain, simple truth

We also saw wisdom passed down through childhood stories that are remembered for a lifetime. Thank you, Mom! These stories carry plain, simple truths that are easily remembered and often retold. In chapter 3 we discussed the importance of a last will and testament, heroes, the necessity of saving capital, how starting early makes a tremendous difference, and planning your affairs for the least amount of taxation. Do not forget our shop owner from Cavendish, PEI, when you are tempted to partially redeem RSP funds for other purposes. "No touch!"

Live within your means

I chose the title of this book from the story in chapter 4 as it is the central message that I wish to convey in this book. *The Lake of Two*

Rivers is an allegory revealing the relationship between income, lifestyle, and wealth. In my opinion, there is nothing more central to personal finance planning than living within your means. We as a country have not done a good job collectively on this as our national debt is a disgrace. Clearly this will translate into much higher marginal tax rates down the road for our children. I hope politicians get to read this, but I am not holding my breath. Shame on them! No, better stated, *shame on us!* Our kids deserve better.

The big white elephant

We went on to some plain, simple truth in chapter 5, explaining the white elephant in the living room is cumbersome, doesn't belong there, is crowding your lifestyle, and possibly is being ignored. That would be at your peril! The only way to eat an elephant is one bite at a time and deliberately, I might add! It has been a continuum of lifestyle exceeding sources of income that has placed the elephant there, not just one or two purchases here or there. We spoke of people's attitude toward their money at the time; it depends greatly on their current bank balance. Placing yourself within an automatic debit, or preauthorized checking plan, often circumvents your temptation to spend those savings. You may need a system of *forced* savings. Don't forget Old Mother Hubbard. It was also mentioned personal finance planning is, for the most part, basic common sense that is just not being practiced. People like to have a big hat.

Financial enemies abound

Chapter 6 was entitled "Financial Enemies," and we alluded to being in a war; this would be financial enemies attacking the wealth you are trying to accumulate. Obvious enemies, such as mortgages and car payments, were quickly pointed out, but there are many others. Depreciation was mentioned, as well as being united in marriage to someone who is a spendthrift or shopaholic. A spendthrift spouse would be very challenging, to say the least. However, many of these enemies are from within our own character. Procrastination was shown to be a good example of this, as well as lack of planning and lack of implementation. I would call these financial diseases as much as financial enemies. So is trading on emotion. Some enemies, such as growing older, are external; we have no control over them whatsoever. We pointed out that by far the worst financial enemy is taxes that are taken from you each year, at three levels of government. For this reason, we dedicated the next full chapter to address this one enemy.

Defer, convert, and avoid!

Slay the dragon. I am not sure if you had envisioned a fire-breathing dragon, but I did. Three simple tools were given you to fight this one enemy, and I hope you remember each of them well. Here they are again, in no particular order of importance: Defer! Don't pay your taxes until you must. Convert! When you convert your growth from income to capital gains and dividends, you have done yourself a tax favor as they are taxed at a much preferable rate. Honorable mention was made of the retirement plans introduced by the government, namely, the Retirement Savings Plan and the Retirement Income Fund, which defer taxes until such time as funds are redeemed. Often in retirement your marginal tax rate is lower. Avoid! Use the existing tax laws to your advantage. If you are not using these plans, why not? That curiosity issue keeps popping up. Not everyone's opinion matches up with truth.

The secret formula

I gave out a secret formula for making money in chapter 8, +PIT, −FIT, which is an acronym for six variables that must be considered to find your true rate of return. You may want to write them down: principal, interest, time, fees, inflation, and taxation. Hopefully the acronym helps you to remember them, for they truly are important if you want to increase your purchasing power. Thirty-five years from now, it may cost you thirty-five dollars to buy a deluxe hamburger. Recall that thirty-five years ago, I bought one for thirty-five cents.

Keep your eyes upon the doughnut

Yes, fees are important, and their effect on your true rate of return also has a compounding effect. However, keep your eyes upon the doughnut and not upon the hole.

Would it not seem appropriate to focus upon factors that affect your result the most?

Footprints in the sand

The story of chapter 9 to me remains poignant. I miss my friend Dave a great deal, and he reminds me yet through his death we are all leaving footprints in the sand. It is ironic he was chiding me not two hours before his own death that I should be aware that anything could happen anytime. He also demonstrated to me in such a vivid form the value of estate planning. It is very important that financial information is recorded for the purpose of your executor. You will not be speaking much at that time. Truly, you have no guarantee of tomorrow.

Think of the whole picture

Chapter 10 reminds us how a close brush with death can cause you to think of what really is important to you. We have needs that exceed financial ones, and you would do well to consider your total needs when planning for your retirement future. Sixteen centuries ago, Socrates recommended we get to know ourselves well. Dr. Maslow has given us a means of ensuring we are thinking of the whole picture. Ignore one of them in your planning, and you may become like the story of our road trip: you are already well down the road, forgot your toothbrush, and there is no turning back.

Life is full of surprises

In chapter 11 we investigated the stress of losing your job. Oftentimes another door of opportunity presents itself; we noted the importance of keeping a positive attitude. Life is full of choices, and little choices made all along the way down the stream can have a dramatic effect on where you end up. The importance of working with a financial advisor has been threaded through all these chapters. Along with lurking financial enemies, many nuances exist out there, some of which you may not be aware. Silly things like government plans must be applied for. Silly things like which pillars upon which you may or may not rely and to what extent you as an individual may rely on each.

Pass it on, pass it on

In the first paragraph of this book, I stated I wished to stick to stories and plain, simple financial truths I have picked up in my life along the way. My goal has been to focus on what really matters to you: happiness in your life and financial success. Perhaps I may have aroused your curiosity on some financial point in your life, or perhaps even something nonfinancial. I consider myself a very, very fortunate man, having had a Wizard of Cause in my life. Perhaps you might consider doing the same for your children, friends, and family. My mission is to be that same wizard to all. This is one of the reasons I have taken the time to write this book.

Wisdom outweighs wealth

In closing, I quote from someone who lived three thousand years ago. No, not the wizard! This man was an actual historical figure and was not only purported to be one of the wealthiest men of his time, he had the fortitude to ask for the gift of wisdom instead of wealth. Like Ozzie, because he asked for a better choice than what most would have asked for, he was granted both. The man was none other than King Solomon. No, this is not me preaching a sermon. It is plain, simple truth. With this final thought I would like to arouse your curiosity. These words are indeed emblazoned on the back of my brain:

Proverbs 21:20

In the house of the wise are many fine wines and oils. But the fool devours all that he has.

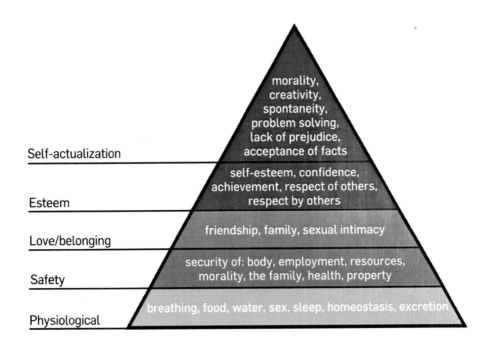

Dr. Abraham Maslow's Hierarchy of Needs

Source:

http://www.google.ca/search?q=maslow's+hierarchy+of+needs&tbm=isch&tbo=u&source=univ&sa=X&ei=sFMNUviDOqit2QXm64GoDQ&sqi=2&ved=0CDUQsAQ&biw=1344&bih=706

This book is dedicated to the memory of:

"The Wizard of Cause"

William Thomas Hopkins

December 25, 1929-November 20, 1999

People, Books, and Companies Index

A

Armstrong, Neil, 37

B

Bohr, Niels, 24
Book of Proverbs (from the Bible), 137
Buffett, Warren, 14-15

C

Chilton, David, 53
Canadian Automobile Association (CAA), 126
Columbus, Christopher, 78

D

Dave (my incognito colleague), 98-105, 135

E

Einstein, Albert, 24
Erickson, Leif, 78

F

Freddie Mac, 18

G

Gretzky, Wayne, 14, 45

H

Heisenberg, Werner, 24
Hopkins, William, 38

K

King, Martin Luther, 37

L

Leibniz, 35

M

Maslow, Abraham, 112-14

N

Newton, Isaac, 35
Nixon, Richard, 37

R

Reagan, Ronald, 37
Regal Capital Planners, 44
Rockel, Paul, 44

S

Shakespeare, William, 104
Socrates, 114
Solomon, 136
Streisand, Barbra, 113

W

Wealthy Barber, The, 53
Wealthy Barber Returns, The, 53

Topic Index

A

acronym for after-tax real rate of return, 38
"Anything can happen anytime," 98, 101, 105, 110
"Ask for help!," 124
asset allocation, 20-21, 44

B

bond rating services, 17, 19
branding of practice, 77, 80
break-even point, 16, 69, 97
business expenses, tax deductible, 82
buy-and-hold strategy, 83
buying dividend-paying funds, 85
buy low, sell high, 23
buy/sell agreement, 99

C

Canada Pension Plan, 113, 128-29
  death benefit, 129
Canadian Deposit Insurance Company, 15
capital gains taxation, 84
carefulness in borrowing money, 70, 123-24
change of attitude, 60, 72
change of habit and preference, 59
commercial paper, 17-18
compound interest, 24-25, 43, 92
  within a tax shelter, 25
continued behavior, 58
"cool and drool " syndrome, 58, 67, 74, 122-23
crystal ball, 19-20, 60
currency devaluation, 54
cycle of life, 111

D

debt, a four-letter word, 54-55, 57, 116
defer, convert, avoid, 88
deferred sales charges (DSCs), 87, 95-96
diversification of your investments, 124
dividend tax, 81
dollar cost averaging, 60-61

E

escheat, 41
estate planning, 41, 76, 104, 107, 111, 129, 135

F

fees, 93
financial enemies
   Canada Revenue Agency, 73, 80
   car payments, 70, 72, 122
   investor emotions, 23, 75, 124, 134
   lack of implementation, 74, 133
   lack of planning, 75, 133
   mortgage, 68-69
   pirates, 67
   procrastination, 74, 133
   spendthrift spouse, 72, 133
   time horizon depletion, 76
financial net worth, 116
forced savings, 60, 62, 133
future value formula, 64

G

guaranteed investment certificates, 15

H

home equity lines of credit, 13

I

important issues, 125-26
inflation, 16-17, 69, 83-84, 90, 93, 96-97, 128
interest, 15, 17-18, 25, 42, 64, 69, 71, 81-83, 85-86, 90-91
interest income, 42, 81, 85-86
intestacy, 57

J

joint executorships, 107

K

key point of this book, 56-57, 65, 133
KISS principle, 11, 62

L

last will and testament, 41, 50, 57, 104
Las Vegas, 22-23, 75
liquidity, 18, 26
living within your means, 53-54, 123, 132
lost money, 15

M

management expense ratios (MERs), 55, 94-95
marginal tax rates, 16, 55, 63, 73, 81-83, 86-87, 133-34
Maslow's hierarchy of needs, 112-14, 135

N

needs in retirement, 111
net savings, 53, 63, 117

O

Old Age Security, 113, 128
one of the great wonders of the world, 24, 64, 92
optimist, 120-21
Ozzie's basic philosophy in life, 33

P

pensions, 129
personal debt, 57
pessimist, 121
plain, simple truth, 56-57, 62, 65, 73-75, 77, 82, 85, 91, 128, 132-33, 136
point of inflection, 111
Ponzi scheme, 12
power of change, 64
power of compounding, 63
power of dreaming, 64, 131
power of observation, 64
power of practicality, 64
power of simplicity, 62
preauthorized checking plan (PAC), 61, 117, 133
principal, 15, 90-91
printing money by the federal reserve, 54
private holdings, 129
probate, 117
purchasing power, 16, 92, 97, 134
purpose of a financial adviser, 12, 20, 74-75, 93, 104-5, 116, 118, 123, 130

R

real, tax-adjusted rate of return, 16
Registered Retirement Savings Plan (RSP), 45, 82, 129
Retirement Income Funds (RIF), 83, 129, 134
retiring line of credit, 65
risk versus return, 15
"Role of an Executor, The," 105
RSP deposits, 82-83

S

savings rule, 43, 45, 60-63, 80, 85, 87, 117, 133
scientific method, 22
second properties, 129
seeking an opinion other than your own, 124
self-actualization, 113-14
selling a business, 129
staying true to your strategy, 124

T

taxation, 16-17, 42, 54, 69, 73, 80-81, 83-86, 93, 96-97, 132, 134
tax deferral within a corporation, 84
tax-free savings accounts (TFSAs), 25, 86
time, 24, 74, 90, 92
truth versus opinion, 97, 111, 126

U

US National Debt, 19

V

various websites, 54-55, 128
Viking pillaging and plundering, 25

W

whole life insurance policies, 129

Edwards Brothers Malloy
Thorofare, NJ USA
September 16, 2013